MW01166692

Pain *Was* My Middle Name

To Dear Lauren,

Best Wishes,

Anita

Pain *Was* My Middle Name

Anita Li Chun
with Eugene Li Chun
and Elaine Li Chun

iUniverse, Inc.
New York Lincoln Shanghai

Pain Was My Middle Name

iUniverse books may be ordered through booksellers or by contacting:

iUniverse
2021 Pine Lake Road, Suite 100
Lincoln, NE 68512
www.iuniverse.com
1-800-Authors (1-800-288-4677)

ISBN-13: 978-0-595-34914-2 (pbk)
ISBN-13: 978-0-595-67167-0 (cloth)
ISBN-13: 978-0-595-79629-8 (ebk)
ISBN-10: 0-595-34914-5 (pbk)
ISBN-10: 0-595-67167-5 (cloth)
ISBN-10: 0-595-79629-X (ebk)

Printed in the United States of America

To Wei Foo, my late husband of fifty-two years, nine months, and eleven days. When I first contemplated writing this book, he was living in oblivion, afflicted with Alzheimer's disease.

CONTENTS

ACKNOWLEDGMENTS

I would like to express my appreciation to Robert Montgomery, my editor. His expertise and enthusiasm for this work go beyond the call of duty.

I also would like to thank all my friends for their great, unequivocal support in my writing of my first book.

INTRODUCTION

Dear Reader,

I would like to express my gratitude to you for your interest in this book. It is, in fact, my honor to share with you my experiences as a victim of rheumatoid arthritis (RA) for over fifty years.

I started writing diaries as a preteen, and it's become a nightly habit. This book is based on fifty-three volumes of my writings.

I am normally a very private person. My original plan was to burn all my diaries before I left this wonderful world. But one day in January 2001, while I was standing in my living room by the statue of Christ on my music cabinet, a very strong message suddenly came to me that I should sacrifice my privacy and write a book about my personal experiences in dealing with rheumatoid arthritis—a book that would document my lifelong mission to improve my condition so I could live a normal and happy life, in spite of its devastation. Most of all, through this book I should share my success with fellow victims of rheumatoid arthritis and other chronic illnesses.

I was apprehensive. I had never written a book or taken a writing course, and English had not been my major. I could see the mountains of work ahead of me. But RA victims are used to mountains! I knew I had to write this book, and I decided then and there to dedicate it to my dear husband, Wei Foo.

This book is written in simple language, almost as if I were chatting with a friend in my living room. The main purpose of this book is to benefit as many victims of RA as possible, and I feel that the simple language enhances my mission.

No disease happens to a general kind of person, but always to a specific individual. I believe RA will only interest you and lead to understanding when you see how it's dealt with in real life.

If you are anything like me, you'd like to know something about the author. For these reasons, I cover some of my background, including family, marriage, and education, in this account. In this way, I hope my life will strike a chord with yours.

CHAPTER 1

THE BEGINNING: THE MYSTERY OF PAIN

It has been a heart-wrenching experience to read through the fifty-three volumes of my diaries and relive some of the darkest days of my life.

* * *

1950. I'm twenty-five, very happily married for a year and a half to a prince of a fellow, and not too far away from my doctorate. On the morning of April 3, I wake Wei up and tell him my arm is very sore. In the bathroom, as he gently rubs Bengay on my arm, I pass out from the excruciating pain. Very frightened, he carries me back to the bed. The pain keeps me there all day, and wakes me at three in the morning. The next day I try heat treatments. The next night I wake up with searing pain in *both* arms.

Our doctor says the pain and unsettled feeling throughout my body mean I'm getting the flu and gives me penicillin. The medicine fixes my temperature, but not the pain. The following nights, I barely sleep, and mornings are even worse. The doctor pays a house call and gives me pain medication. It only helps a little, and I don't want to take too much for fear of the side effects.

April 11. The pain starts moving around wherever it pleases. One day my left wrist and right leg burn like crazy. The next day my right wrist throbs so much I worry more and more every minute. The next night, the pain in my left shoulder and arm is so bad that I'm afraid to move. The next day my right elbow and fingers feel as if they're being cut from the inside. Sometimes the pain moves to the weirdest places—like my jaw.

I am spending more time at the doctor's office than I do in my own house. From the way the pain moves, the doctor says it's rheumatism. The damp April weather seems to make it worse. He continues to give me penicillin when my temperature goes up, but the pain medication and sleeping pills don't really help much. The pain seems to burrow through my body without mercy and is at times very severe. As for finishing my studies, forget about it—the pain is too much.

Symptoms of Rheumatoid Arthritis (RA)

- **Pain, stiffness, swelling, and loss of joint function**
- **Fatigue**
- **Low-grade fever**
- **Loss of appetite**
- **Weight loss**

Symptoms can vary from individual to individual and can change from day to day.

Finally, after fifty days, the rheumatism seems to have left me. I pray to God that it never comes back again. My doctor gives me my last injection of penicillin and vitamins. He's happy that he won't have to see my beautiful face so often.

June–July. It's back. I don't understand, Lord, but please give me strength.

My arms, legs, and fingers get the first round, then my left wrist won't let me sleep, then my shoulders and toes start to scream, and on it goes. I try aspirin. The pain laughs at my futile attempts to remove it.

I'm hungry all the time. Is that the rheumatism too? The doctor gives me blood tests. In July, he tells me I'm pregnant. Good news at last—thank the Lord! The doctor wants me to rest a great deal and curtail my activities, even cooking, to avoid a miscarriage like the one I had last October. My symptoms worry him. He wants to be sure I can hold my baby. (I do, too!)

August. I'm the *opposite* of hungry. I see doctors so much I feel I'm on a merry-go-round. My rheumatism fluctuates. At times it's tolerable (Wei and I even see a movie); other times it's terrible (burning elbows and shoulder, extremely swollen ankles and feet). One night one finger hurts so badly that I can't sleep all night. Another morning I wake to find my left big toe the size of a walnut. My temperature rises. My hemoglobin lowers. On it goes, but I can't stop knitting things for my coming baby.

October–December. So much is happening! My parents move from Hong Kong to live in our apartment building. My baby swims around inside me. I vomit in the night. Was it the liver I had for dinner?

I've heard that pregnancy can make signs of rheumatism disappear. I guess I'm not one of the lucky ones. My swollen feet hurt so much that I can hardly walk, but I go out a lot—to see doctors. Injections, examinations, and urine tests are my new social activities.

Still, I manage to cook a Thanksgiving turkey for seven. Everyone in my wonderful family helps, and I feel very thankful to God for all our blessings, even though my joints are inflamed and aching and at times unbearably painful.

And thank God for music! I still play the piano, and all through December, I hum and sing to my growing baby. My lack of sleep from the rheumatism must be affecting me, however, because the words come out funny:

> *Young Mrs. McChun had some pain,*
> *Ee-yow, ee-ow ee!*

On December 31, I write in my diary: "The past year I have not been too healthy, but I am happy! Happy New Year!"

1951. Knitting, sewing, doctor visits, shopping for baby stuff, preparing the apartment for the blessed arrival, having my parents around—all very exciting, but the pain never stops. What can I do? *March forth!* That's what I do. On March 4, 1951, we rush through the red lights to the hospital at dawn, and our beautiful son, Eugene, is born into the world.

Seven pounds, nineteen inches, healthy, good-looking, and *hungry!* Wei and I are in Heaven. There are many visitors. My room looks like a florist's. Baby Eugene is the first grandchild for Wei's mother and father. I am grateful to God for this special blessing. If only I could lose the rheumatism, I'd be the luckiest woman on Earth.

We can only afford a baby nurse for my first three weeks at home. My pain is unbelievable, but being a new mother gives me the strength I need to make it.

May. I can't sleep, rest, or put weight on my tender feet for long, but I walk and even jump at times for Eugene. He is so cute! When he is two months old, lying on my bed, he laughs out loud. Can you believe it?

June. My feet are in such agony. I soak them in Epsom salts, rub them with wintergreen, and warm them with a heat lamp. The doctor prescribes thiamin, then salicylate pills, which help, but they also upset my stomach. Wei has to take many days off from work when the pain interferes with my childcare. My days are a strange mixture of extreme suffering and extreme joy with Eugene. My parents help when I need them, but they never did domestic work in China and are starting a new life in their sixties.

To encourage myself, I read about great people who overcame sicknesses. This gives me inspiration, but I'm very disgusted by my illness. In addition, the pain is still a mystery to the doctor. This is the worst part. Since he can't do more than give me injections (of vitamins, basically), I visit a rheumatologist.

CHAPTER 2

THE VERDICT

1951, July: I make an appointment to see Dr. R., the rheumatologist. He draws 10cc of my blood for tests. A few days later, I go for X-rays and radioactive tests at the medical center. I still have lots of pain, particularly in my feet. At times, there are cramps and tingling all over my legs. It is very uncomfortable, to say the least.

July 17. Wei takes a half-day off to go with me to see Dr. R. The verdict is in. Doctor R. has reviewed my blood tests and X-rays. Now he looks in my eyes and gives me the diagnosis I dread the most: *rheumatoid arthritis.*

I have been reading about this disease. Very little is known at this time. It's a chronic disorder of unknown origin, probably hereditary. It causes painful swelling, stiffness in the joints, and loss of joint function. Worst of all, there is no cure. The sentence is life imprisonment with increasing pain, crippling deformities, and premature death, usually from the side effects of the drugs prescribed. Doctor R. is optimistic, though. He advises me to try the prescription for two weeks at least and see how it helps.

Facts about RA

- **RA can occur in both children and adults, but symptoms usually appear in middle age.**
- **Three times more women have RA than men.**
- **RA is an autoimmune disorder. In RA, the victim's own immune system attacks the synovial membrane lining the joints.**
- **More than 2.1 million people suffer from RA in the United States.**
- **No cure has been found for RA, and most sufferers experience lifelong symptoms.**

On the way home, I remember how just a few years ago my friends and I climbed the stairs of the Statue of Liberty and gazed out of her eyes, none of us the least out of breath. I felt as if I were standing on top of the world that day. The grand expanse of Manhattan stretched northward. Boats glided along the harbor, looking like toys. I glimpsed the tablet with "July 4, 1776" etched in Roman numerals in Lady Liberty's left hand. Will I ever again have the physical strength to enjoy such a grand view of life?

All my dreams have been shattered.

I manage to control my emotions all day, but at night, I completely break down. All I can see is a dark future lit only by the fire of pain. Wei, as always, is so considerate, comforting, gently encouraging, and optimistic.

July 18. I've never been this depressed. Why don't I just leave this world? Forgive me, Lord, but I feel I need more than blind faith right now. I know it would be most un-Christian to take my own life, but where's the good news in this dreaded disease? I know I have blessings; I can't deny that. My devoted husband and my precious child really make up for the short end of the stick my life seems to have become. Suicide would only burden them and all my dear friends and family with sadness. I cannot even bear to think about it. Besides, can I leave my baby to the mercy of another woman? Could I let another woman raise my son?

No.

My love for Wei and Eugene outweighs rheumatoid arthritis. I've never been a coward. Why should I start now?

I must fight this disease in every way I can and survive to live a useful and meaningful life.

July 19–24. The prescription lessens my pain a lot but makes me tired and queasy. Wei has taken over the chores so I can rest more. He's more wonderful than I can describe. With his support, I know I can make it. We make a point to keep up with our friends. I won't be an invalid and live like a hermit. What good would that do?

July 25. The pain is back with a vengeance. Almost all my joints ache at the same time! I lie frozen, agonizing over whether to move. Even turning my head a tiny bit to the left fills me with a thousand knives of regret.

Doctor R. wants me in the hospital for further tests and treatment.

End of July. I share a semiprivate room with a middle-aged woman, Mrs. J. She has severe RA but is never grouchy, and we have become friends.

Doctor R. is now wondering if what I have is actually rheumatoid arthritis. Is he kidding me?

These new white pills they're giving me—why won't they tell me what they are?—relieve the pain a lot. That's good news, at least.

A new nurse finally tells me that they're cortisone. That's bad news. I confront the doctor. How can I reduce the dosage? I can't take them forever. He says not to be alarmed; he's had many cases where they help remarkably.

I worry about side effects but revel in having pain that's mild and not severe like it has been. I love how happy Wei is to see me feeling better. I go home and cry when I see my baby again. I missed him so much!

August–October. Into everyone's life, a little sunshine must fall. Wei and I dance and dance at his fraternity reunion—just like the old days. Thank God, I'm feeling happy and normal again because so much is happening! A stream of family visits my parents and us. The baby grows in leaps and bounds. I study to be a citizen. We're looking for a larger home. I'm taking the cortisone miracle drug off and on.

Then hay fever wipes me out.

My hay fever pills make me groggy, as if I'm just waking up from anesthesia. My doctor gives me new pills but asks me to stop the cortisone. The pain returns. It's severe, but not quite unbearable. It exhausts me to take Eugene to the park, but it makes him happy. I keep up with my knitting, sewing, and mahjong. I encourage Wei to have bowling nights with his buddies. In addition, every Saturday, I go the extra mile and visit his family for dinner.

Ever since we learned I had rheumatoid arthritis, Wei's mother has treated me like damaged goods. I like his father; he's a jolly guy. He likes me too, as does most of the family. People generally like me.

But Wei's mama stares daggers at me. She sits with the corners of her mouth turned down, aiming her small, hate-filled eyes at me. She is not stable, my mother-in-law. She has no friends or education of which to speak. She seems close to a breakdown all the time; her family bends backward to keep her appeased. She envies the special attention that Wei—her firstborn—gives to me. This is not right, but what can I do? I certainly can do without the stress of her venom. It makes my RA worse.

One visit I decide to stare daggers back at her! We stare and we stare and we don't make a sound. I wonder how long she'll hold out. Finally, she blinks and looks down. My eyes are much bigger than hers, and so are the daggers, I guess. This episode seems to cure her staring habit considerably. She still makes unpleasant remarks to me and badmouths me behind my back. If she were my *stepmother*-in-law, I'd end that, too. But I am properly brought up, and for Wei's sake, I treat her with respect.

Nevertheless, it's awful how some people—especially at this point in time—blame rheumatoid arthritis on the sufferer—as if we don't have enough problems! Even some doctors and psychiatrists—too proud to say they don't know—say that it's probably just in the mind. When I first heard this theory, I got all excited, thinking I could cure myself. Little did I know, and they knew less.

November–December. I'm becoming an American! My initiation to the red, white, and blue is the endless *red* tape and *white* paper. I fill out for forms and tests, and how *blue* I get from hurrying to Ellis Island all the time just to wait around for hours—but it's worth it! I'm exhausted but proud. Celebrations follow, including my twenty-seventh birthday and our third anniversary.

Eugene says "mama" and "papa" and is already walking sure-footedly. The doctor declares his development advanced in every aspect.

My father cooks a great Christmas dinner and is happy beyond words because his grandson loves his first Christmas tree.

CHAPTER 3

SEARCHING FOR A CURE

1952. A year of cortisone, on and off, gives me not only relief but also palpitations and restlessness. Doctor R. is still optimistic about my condition, but I really don't believe him.

Wei works late many evenings. The little one misses his daddy when night comes. Still, I manage taking care of him by myself pretty well. I keep sewing and knitting in my spare time. It's enjoyable to me. The pain is ever-present, but it can't take away how much I love my life, thank God. Eugene is growing and easier to care for, except for his teething bouts, which increase my sleepless nights. Wei and I are enjoying each other, our friends, and our new blue, two-tone, four-door Ford sedan that we bought for $2,400.

Our next-door neighbor thinks food allergies are linked to arthritis and suggests cutting salt from my diet. Years later, I read in the newspaper that tests have linked arthritis to food allergies. A simple diet change can bring relief to arthritics. This tiny seed my neighbor plants in me grows into a healing garden of knowledge—knowledge of how deeply diet relates to RA.

Occasionally, I go shopping. That makes me feel good about myself (but not my feet). Even with the constant pain, I do not feel depressed. In fact, I am quite happy most of the time.

However, the September hay fever season pushes the pain over the edge. I have to take PBZ tablets for relief from the hay fever. Sometimes I get so low. I feel as if something's missing inside me. I pray every night for strength. Wei and I discuss moving west to a drier climate, but Dr. R. thinks the chances that it would help are not worth the upheaval in our lives.

Christmas. Eugene meets Santa and is completely fascinated! The big guy he adores the most, however, is my father. I love my father very much, and to watch them smell the Christmas tree together fills me with joy. I go to the piano and play "Joy to the World."

1953. The "gold" year. To wean me from cortisone, Dr. R. starts giving me gold injections. I'm praying it works. A plastic hand mold now aids my circulation at night, but the awful unsettled feeling still shrieks in my legs, scaring sleep away. I am rather discouraged. I call Mrs. J., my roommate at the hospital who has very severe RA. She reports she's left Dr. R. and is down to two aspirins a day with her new doctor, who uses unconventional treatments, such as metal coils wrapped around areas of the body. *Hmm,* I think. I'm having very bad reactions to the gold injections, but Dr. R. is telling me that's a good sign, meaning it will work later on. *Hmm,* I think again. More injections. My lips blister. My face, already puffy from the cortisone, now has a terrible rash that starts spreading. Enough *hmm.* I'm hospitalized.

I suffer through long intravenous infusions (PBZ and ACTH) to counter my bad gold reaction. Some are so painful that people have to hold me up to keep me from falling over. Wei's mother says her family's too busy to visit, and another family member spreads the story that it's all in my head. My rash improves a little, and Dr. R. offers me as a special case of someone hyper-allergic to gold to a group of doctors. This prolongs my stay while they try out further treatments: cortisone by mouth, excruciating BAL injections. I'm their guinea pig! I'm a nice lady, but my anger is about to erupt like a volcano. They finally let me out after nine days.

The rash gets a lot better, but the injections continue, and so does the awful, unbearable itching. A hundred boils emerge all over my body. When they break open, pus pours out—it's like striking oil. I'm so miserable. If I had a pistol, I'd do something unthinkable. Doctor R. seems kind of frightened of me. *Hmm.* I call Mrs. J.'s unconventional doctor.

His name is Dr. K. I like him. He answers our thousand questions and gives Wei and me a good feeling. Many of his patients tell me encouraging stories. He takes me off fruit and milk to eliminate allergenic gas. For my first treatment, he puts a net of spring coils on my back, which I lay on for almost three hours. The next day goes by without any pain, even though it's damp April weather. The next day I do all the cleaning and ironing and still do not feel any pain. It's like magic!

I continue to see Dr. K. on Saturdays. The treatments take many hours, but they work. Everyone's impressed. I'm totally off cortisone and Bufferin. I see Dr. R. for penicillin for my boils, which are slowly leaving my body. Doctor R. sees me doing so well and thinks he's the one doing such wonders for me. When I finally tell him in June that it's Dr. K.'s metal therapy doing the trick, he calls him a phony and a quack.

Nevertheless, I'm *feeling* golden now—and not the fool's gold Dr. R. gave me. I still have little problems in my feet, but Dr. K. suggests arches. I have them made and they help. I shop downtown in two-inch heels for the first time in I don't know how long! My hay fever problems are also improving. I'm also happy to find I can play the piano without pain in my wrists.

One June evening, as Wei and I take a peaceful stroll down Riverside Drive, I tell him it would make me very happy if he and Eugene would get baptized together and become Christians. "If it makes you happy, your wish will come true," he answers. I tell him he can't just do it for me, but he has to honestly believe in God and Christ. He nods in that special, quiet way he has. He begins to go to church and listen to sermons with me.

In August, we spend a great week in the Poconos, our first family vacation. In September, Eugene starts nursery school and takes to it like a fish to water. It is so, so gratifying to see him enjoy the school and his classmates so much. He's an outstanding boy in every way. What a blessing to have this precious little guy as our son!

In November, I take driving lessons and practice with Wei in the evening. These are nice times. By Christmas, my father's recovered from his ulcer, and at our New Year's Eve party, I play "Auld Lang Syne."

1954, January. I get my driver's license but still enjoy the newfound ease of walking.

We have given up the idea of moving to the suburbs due to the long hours of commuting for Wei. I'm just thinking, maybe there's a place within walking distance. You never know. It won't hurt to look, and walking is always good exercise! I take a walk to see whether there's a building in which we would maybe like to live.

Besides, I have a feeling. One of those light feelings you get that makes breathing seem like a prayer. We're in God's hands, are we not? I'm just taking another peaceful stroll down Riverside Drive.

I see a building I like. I go in and talk to the super. He likes me. Later in the month, I get a call.

It's the super, with super news.

He has a large apartment ready for the taking. We take it! Six rooms, just two blocks away! It's a godsend. (Fifty years later, I'm now writing this book in that same beautiful apartment.)

February–September. The godsend needs a lot of work! I help move, I sew drapes, I paint, I scrape, and I get new furniture. I'm seeing Dr. K. every other week now, but one day my wrist goes ballistic and cramps up in crippling pain. No matter what Dr. K. attempts, it gets worse. He insists he can cure me, but I know the magic is gone. Making a truly agonizing decision, I stop seeing Dr. K.

in September, after forty-seven treatments. The wife of someone Wei works with highly recommends another doctor, and I make an appointment.

October–December. Doctor P.'s office is on Park Avenue. He believes that to fight arthritis, one has to fight the force of gravity. He fits a padded metal belt around my pelvis to deflect the pull of gravity from my body. There go my tight Chinese dresses!

He suggests low heels and deep breathing to relax the body: one beat in, three beats out. The more rested and stressless the body becomes, the better it works to fight painful intrusions. This truth will serve me with increasing power the rest of my life.

His office treatments are massage and metal therapies, twice a week at first, and he's not exactly cheap. But I'm not as tired as before, and I'm still off cortisone. Sometimes he injects me with calcium. After treatment number four, he tells me that soon I'll be getting a charley-horse feeling all over my body. That's normal, he says, and lasts just four days, and then there will be one more, half as bad. Easy for him to say!

Nevertheless, he's right, and in two months, I'm able again to be really active, which is just how I like it. When Wei and his friends build bookshelves, I'm the one filling them up with books. I volunteer at Eugene's school and at Sunday services and have dinner with my parents more and more often. Eugene loves them, and he brings such joy to their autumn years. He favors his grandpa, whom he calls Baunka because he can't say grandpa. In addition, it just so happens that Grandpa is a banker! Eugene even feeds grapes to Baunka when Baunka is still asleep on the couch! When Baunka argues with my mother, Eugene goes over and gives her a little kick, to show whose side he's on.

I'm doing very well with my RA these days. I'm only on medication occasionally, when certain joints act up. Even then I just take over-the-counter pain relievers for a short period until the flare-up ends. I'm very happy with the improvement.

In November, Wei's former principal suggests I join his life insurance business. He could train me, and I could work from home at my own pace. This is great. Even though I'm down to once a week with Dr. P., the money would really come in handy. I also like this kind of work. I have a head for business. I say yes, and the year ends.

1955. Even in the bad years, there's always plenty of good. I'm sworn in as a citizen in May, my life insurance trainer raves about my progress, and—when Dr. P. goes on vacation—I still do very well. My RA doesn't slow me down when I get the rest I need.

My father has a heart attack in November. The doctor prescribes a heart-friendly diet and rest, and Dad does well following this regimen. President

Eisenhower's quick recovery from his heart attack a month ago makes us optimistic. In December, however, my father also has major ulcer surgery. He stays with us to recuperate. I'm from a large family, and many come to visit and are always around. Cooking, cleaning, phone calls, doctors, tending Dad, and worrying—I'm fine as long as I can rest enough. But I can't.

1956. Ike is reelected, but my father's health declines. He has surgery on his intestines twice in the first three months and recuperates in our apartment. In addition to caring for him, I also have to telephone and cable updated reports of his health to the rest of the family (scattered throughout America and China). I'm not doing badly considering the lack of rest.

I have nine treatments from Dr. P. in these first three months of the year. Our cleaning lady sometimes babysits for us. Eugene is very busy attending nursery and Sunday school and playing with his numerous friends. We have his friends over often, and I take him to the park when the weather permits. I want no traumatic change for him because of his grandfather's illness. Wei starts an intense course to prepare for his architect license examination, spending many evening hours at school. I'm also looking at elementary schools for Eugene, and I find a good one. He has to go through many tests and interviews to enter kindergarten in September.

The year 1956 turns out to be a very heartbreaking, strenuous year for me because of my dear father's ill health. He keeps getting hospitalized for either heart attacks or heart failure. My sisters, brothers, sister-in-law, and nephews are here off and on. There are big meals to cook, hospital visits, and consultations with the doctors. All the duties, plus telephone calls and cablegrams to the siblings who were not here—it's all wearing down my health. I never seem to get enough sleep.

Four heart attacks and three surgeries in ten months—Father's body finally surrenders. He dies peacefully in the hospital, July 1 at 9:45 AM. My siblings flock from the Orient, California, and Michigan with their children. I take care of accommodations and last arrangements through great pain and grief. It's very sad for us all, particularly little Eugene. He's subdued but full of questions. When told that Baunka is in Heaven, he asks, "Is it okay if I throw something up there?" And when he sees how sad his grandmother is, he goes over and hugs her leg.

My father was a remarkable man. He was born in 1888, the son of a protestant minister whose paternal grandmother converted to Christianity and held our family together. My father was the apple of this great woman's eye because of his intelligence and good looks.

Inspired by his grandmother and his devout family, he left China for the University of Chicago on a full scholarship, the only way he could afford such a venture. While earning his BA, he supported himself working cold Windy City nights in a Chinese restaurant. (In later years, he always got a kick out of showing his children how to carry a tall stack of dishes on one arm.)

After graduation, he stayed just long enough to earn back the scholarship money, which he then gave to the university as a fund for another deserving student. Then he returned to Shanghai and prospered in a number of businesses.

His favorite work was with stocks and bonds. He loved to analyze corporations and their worth, and in time became a director of a major private bank. My brother Richard, a graduate of Harvard—which my father called "the University of Chicago of the East"—would one day become the president of the same bank.

My mother was handpicked for my father by his adoring grandmother, and the marriage was fruitful—he raised a family of eleven (I was number nine). Radically ahead of his time, especially for China, he treated his four daughters as equals to his sons. He wanted *all* his children to have fine educations to insure we had the resources we needed in changing times and to broaden our horizons so we'd more deeply appreciate life's blessings.

His hands-on Christian compassion still inspires me today. Poor relatives, needy friends, people without jobs, worthy charities—all knew that if they came to him, they'd be helped.

One day when I was a teenager, he asked me to take a large donation to an orphanage. The American lady who greeted me was ecstatic. She lifted the cover from a large barrel and gestured me to look. I peered in and saw only a few grains of rice scattered on the bottom. Nearly in tears, she told me how hard she'd been praying because she didn't know how she could feed her children the next meal, and this was truly a miracle from the Lord!

I'll never forget that beautiful American lady and that bare rice barrel, and this miracle my father planted in my heart. When years later, I gave money to a fellow student too poor to get enough food, my father was so proud of me. I couldn't have been happier. He even encouraged me to help more needy students and offered me extra funds to do so. This was my amazing father!

When the Communists took over China, it was dangerous for prosperous people. Some of my father's friends took their own lives to avoid torture and interrogation. My parents abandoned sizable holdings to escape to Hong Kong and eventually came to New York City, virtually starting over with a new language and a new citizenship. It was a simpler life for my father, full of family pleasures and the trials of aging, but he continued to remain an expert on the stock market as well as a master at pleasing children!

It was such a blessing to be my father's daughter. I thank God for this good fortune!

After he leaves us, however, after all the last arrangements, after every relative goes home, I seem to become allergic to everything! Wool, toothpaste, cosmetics, and lotion—almost anything I touch except for Ivory soap.

It took two years for this condition to gradually fade. What I'm most allergic to, I think, is my father not being around anymore. It's the touch of his generous hands I miss.

Yet I'm still able to keep the life he and mother gave me active and full. I collect money door-to-door for arthritis and rheumatism foundations, work almost daily for my son's school, take him to the circus or rodeo or movies with his cousins and little school friends, go with friends to Broadway shows and church events—including dancing in high heels at a cotillion and doing a fashion show in a Chinese dress (without the gravitron!)—and continue to chip away at my father's estate matters.

I still get tired easily, and continue my treatments with Dr. P., though not as often as last year. I'm taking cod liver oil now (makes me gag unless I take it with juice, but works so well), and I'm looking more into diet to improve my condition. Wei is working intensely for his architect license, and in October I resume the insurance training I put on hold when father took ill.

At Christmastime, Eugene asks for a special little tree for Grandpa and decorates it all by himself. Every time we look at it, we think of my father, each in our own way. The little guy really misses his pal. It's been a sad year, but full of God's mysterious blessings.

1957–1963. From the age of thirty-two to thirty-eight, rheumatoid arthritis continues to hurt me as I forge through my busy days. Some spells are less severe, and I go some months without Dr. P. Sooner or later, the aggressive misery returns, and pain clearly becomes my middle name again.

There are mornings when Wei has to pull me from the front as my son's little hands push on my back just to get me out of the bed. They are always so kind to me—it's for them that I get up; it's for them that I pray for more strength and struggle to live a normal life.

So far we are succeeding.

Wei begins to show a real interest in religion, and we become regular churchgoers and read spiritual books. Then he and Eugene get baptized together. The minister says it's the first time in his entire ministry he baptized a father and son together.

I remain a very happy person even though my RA never leaves me. Wei gets his architect license. I become an insurance agent and a mutual funds representative. Because of my job, we can afford wonderful vacations and camp for Eugene, which he loves and where he excels.

Where does the time go? One day I'm playing piano for him and his friends and he's playing along on toy instruments. Then he's suddenly eleven, playing "Moon River" on a guitar for the entire summer camp (to long applause)!

Even Wei's mother starts accepting that her son has found a good life with someone who is not damaged goods. She still makes unpleasant remarks from time to time, but I'm told that her criticisms of me behind my back are now mixed with praises too. We all understand it's her nature. She's a very lonely woman. She eventually gets sick with extreme depression and asks me to pray for her. I'm puzzled and overwhelmed by this complete turnabout in her attitude toward me. I guess she knows how much I rely on prayer. Whatever the reason, I believe it's God's work, and of course I pray for her.

My doctor knows that I would like to have another child. Now my doctor tells me my health is good enough to have my wish. It's very hard for me to decide whether or not to have another child. It's one of the hardest decisions of my life. I'm thirty-seven years old, carrying the burden of a grim disease, and prone to tiredness and uncertain health with a very busy family and professional life. Taking such good care of myself has led me to this challenging possibility. I pray every night over this decision—many nights. In addition, I wake up one morning with the feeling of a prayer answered, the feeling of *yes!* I decide to have another child.

The hardest decision of my life turns out to be the best.

I can't tell you how many times I thank God for the wisdom of this decision!

My own mother, on a very exciting day in August of 1962, proudly becomes a U.S. citizen.

However, a few weeks later she's diagnosed with kidney cancer.

Once again, I begin the grim routine of long distance calls and cables to all the siblings to keep them up-to-date on her health. I accompany her to the hospital for long hours of tests and examinations. I'm still busy with my own work during this time of great stress, constant activity, and demanding responsibilities. It is truly a trying time for my soul.

I go with her to the hospital for her operation so she won't be too frightened. I spend all day there. The operation takes hours longer than expected. They successfully remove her right kidney and her ureter, which were 99 percent cancerous.

In the following days of recovery, I make more phone calls and spend long hours in the less-than-refreshing atmosphere of the hospital. I'm also cooking her chicken broth and noodles every day because—like most people—she doesn't like hospital food. I always start with a fresh chicken because my mother is very particular. These days you can always smell the aroma of chicken broth cooking on my stove. I'm happy to see her eating more and more each day.

After twenty-four days, she comes to our place for recuperation. Eugene offers his room for Grandma and moves to the small room in the back. He's always such a kind and thoughtful little fellow, and he truly loves his grandma. I find a nice Chinese lady to help me care for Mother (mostly to keep her company). After two months of all this tender loving care and medical attention, she's able to travel to California to my sister's place. Her recovery is complete.

It's a great relief because—in addition to all the stress and worry, the accommodations and visiting, the phone calls, the hostessing, the cooking, the working, and the RA—I'm also pregnant!

As the due date draws closer, my prayer changes to: *If it's another boy, Lord, I accept—but you know I want a little girl.* I even begin to pray for the face I want to see on this child! Then, March 11, 1963, our little Elaine enters the world. Our tiny princess!

She has the face I prayed for.

Could a mother ever adore a face more? Even Wei's mother says she's the most beautiful baby she's ever seen in her life. My prayers for my mother-in-law seem to have improved her powers of observation!

Like her brother, Elaine laughs out loud at two months—though hers is more of a giggle. What is it with my babies that they laugh so soon? It must be my funny face.

I'm grateful my RA is not too bad in pregnancy, and the delivery is relatively easy. I'm taking mega-vitamins now (mostly C, D, E, and calcium), cod liver oil, some over-the-counter pain pills, and treatments with Dr. P. as needed.

In 1959 I also discover the Niagara Thermo Massage Pad, which relaxes me enough, thank God, to get out of bed without that ridiculous business of my family pushing and pulling on me. For the rest of my life, this massage pad will be a special blessing to me.

Nevertheless, the long nights (Elaine was not a sleeper) and care of the precious new baby happen along with a terrible flare-up of RA. In too many dark hours, I find myself wondering how I will survive. I feel I'm living day-by-day and pray to live until Elaine's tenth birthday so at least she'll know her mother that long. By April, my hands and my feet feel as if I'm holding and walking on red-hot blades.

Dr. P. puts me on NSAID pills (nonsteroidal anti-inflammatory drugs). I enter the hospital for two weeks in June for surgery on both of my feet to correct the bunions. This is the first of many operations I will have over the years to correct arthritic deformities. The surgery is a success, but my RA keeps behaving badly. Still, I manage to help get Eugene packed and sent off to camp in New Hampshire. He helps a lot; he's a very neat little packer.

We hire a young woman from the South to help with the baby. She's twenty and conscientious, but turns out to be immature and unreliable in the end. She stays for just three months, and when she goes I find I can manage very well without her. My arthritis is giving me maddening pain, but I still do a hundred turns every morning on the Exercycle—quite a chore!

In addition, one day, paging through *Look* magazine, what do I find? It is a story of Dr. L. in Canada, with an impressive new treatment for rheumatoid arthritis. I write him, he writes back immediately, and a week later, I'm heading for Canada and a brand-new world.

CHAPTER 4

FINDING THE BEST PARTIAL CURES

1963, early September. I meet with Dr. L. and think: What a nice man and good doctor this guy is! Dr. L. looks elegant and confident. He greets me warmly. He is a good listener and puts me at ease during our discussion of my condition. I have the feeling that I can trust him and that he will help me. I also like how amazed he is at my health after thirteen years of RA.

I pray over whether I should begin treatments with him and find the answer in my good feelings for him. I put drops of his liquid medicine (hormones and prednisone) under my tongue at varying times every day. He assures me there will be no side effects, but my policy is always to take the smallest amount of any medicine and reduce it if I can.

Late September–December. Doctor L.'s medicine works dramatically. Even after lowering the dosage several times, I don't feel dragged down by pain—even in humid weather. I get rid of my NSAID pills, quickly make some big insurance sales, and even weather a tax audit! I survive sleepless nights when Elaine is teething and bake hundreds of cookies for Eugene's school dance.

Then I become anemic with low blood pressure. A vitamin injection fixes me up, however. I thank God it's not Dr. L.'s wonderful medicine that's the problem. My Christmas bustles with activity. My life is so busy, and I enjoy it so much. On New Year's Eve, we're invited to four parties that keep us hopping until four in the morning.

The year 1963 is challenging and full of change. With the Lord looking over us, things somehow work out beautifully with the birth of my daughter and the great improvement in my health.

1964–1966. I continue to see Dr. L. periodically, flying to and from Montreal, usually all in one day.

Each precious year flies as fast as that plane, it seems, and Dr. L. and his medicine fortify me well for all the ups and downs. Mother's health begins to fail, even as my children bloom with life. At the age of one, Elaine loves to wiggle and laugh like crazy to the Flying Nun song. It's no wonder she's picked up the pet name "Suzie Cute." At sixteen months, she sees a ballet on TV, and immediately she walks on her toes, dances around, and starts taking bows! My handsome, athletic son enters his teens as a leader in school and camp. ("It's nice," he says, "to have two kinds of life: summer and winter, country and city.") He forms a band that plays at all sorts of functions. It's no ordinary band of young musicians—they actually get paid! In addition, Wei leaves his job of ten years to form a partnership with a colleague in a Greenwich Village office, of which I heartily approve. Wei is much more relaxed and happier—this is an answer to our prayers. In no time at all, they land a big project.

I am still constantly suffering from RA (some days worse than others), but Dr. L.'s treatments keep it from laying me up and stabilize it so I can manage and make plans. His medicine is a lifesaver, but I continue to keep my daily doses to a minimum. I add calcium and magnesium to my daily vitamins and then start adding others. I'm very careful to notice what helps and what doesn't. Cold, damp, or stormy weather still makes my joints hurt. I still play the piano and sew quite a bit: drapes, bedspreads, Elaine's clothes, and my own casual wear. I even clean the Venetian blinds in the bathtub—that's quite a job! Then there's my insurance business, doing tax returns, being the coordinating parent for Eugene's school class, keeping up with my jump-for-joy daughter (she starts half-day Montessori school in September), and all the church activities. Ordinary life is extraordinarily busy!

Then there is the fabulous New York World's Fair, which we go to. (I can't tell you how many times!) Our little girl loves it, particularly a boat ride named "It's a Small World," with little people everywhere singing and scampering around. So many friends and relatives come to stay with us to see the fair that we sometimes ask our neighbors to accommodate them. It is a lot of fun. Even my mother comes to enjoy the fair and stays with us four months. She loves it, and it's good to have this time with her.

1967. My brother J. moves to Manhattan, two blocks from us, to take a job with *The New York Times.* Then mother goes into the hospital for a blood clot, and they find inoperable cancer. I cook her lunch and dinner every day and bring it to the hospital (she won't eat hospital food). I sew her gowns of very fine cotton (hospital gowns make her itchy), and launder and iron her fresh ones each day. J. and I look at a nursing home and decide that's not the solution.

We set up J.'s apartment with a hospital bed and other equipment. We also employ two twelve-hour shifts of nurses. An ambulance brings mother to live there.

I continue to bring her lunch and dinner and do her daily laundry. To keep her as comfortable as possible, her pain medication increases. It is the most devastating experience, watching her get worse and completely unable to help. She passed away on December 8 in the morning, freed from all her pain and suffering, and her face had a look of great peace.

My mother was a much-loved woman with her own stories to tell: her girlhood in China, her marriage to my father, having eleven children, and escaping persecution. She had a lot of courage. She came to America separately from my father, with cards that had Chinese on one side and English on the other that she would show to people when she needed to communicate. She spent many hours on hard school benches taking night classes in English, and she earned her American citizenship. Even in her sixties, she did what she could to ease the burdens I had from RA, whether it was baby-sitting or simple acts of kindness. She was a grandmother the kids will never forget.

I choose a bronze casket for her that is identical to Father's, and she is laid to rest by his side.

New Year's Eve is a quiet one. Wei and I go to church. I pray for my departed parents and thank God for holding me up. These are very dark hours.

1968. The ordeal of my mother dying—the stress, the hosting, the arrangements, and the grief—has not only put great pain in my heart but also in my hands and feet. I need all her courage and my family's love just to go on. I get help with the cleaning, I become chairperson of Eugene's class, and I find I can even play the piano when Elaine and her friends want to sing. Then I find out Dr. L.'s license has been suspended, his office raided, and all his medicine confiscated. Doctor L. has been accused of dispensing harmful medicine to his patients. In reality, the legal proceedings themselves are hurting me! I try to ration what I have left, but the pain badly curtails my life. I'm taking the normal dose because of the pain, and I join with Dr. L.'s patients to get a top-notch attorney.

1969, January. I'm learning more how diet helps my condition. I've cut out dairy (but not butter), citrus, and most starches. It helps! Eugene, who is now driving, gets accepted at the University of Michigan. My sister lives there with her family, so I have peace of mind for any emergency Eugene might face. That helps too!

February. I'm going to be a witness at Dr. L.'s trial. I compile facts and records from my ongoing diaries and fly to Montreal.

I'm the second witness called, and swearing on the Bible to tell the truth makes me feel right at home. I testify that Dr. L.'s techniques have been nothing but helpful for me. Later I'm told—with my diaries and confidence—I made a very strong witness. Doctor L. is found not guilty. His medicine is once more available to all of us RA victims. Thanks to the Lord from whom all blessings flow and to my fellow sufferers and all you who help us.

Once more I return to the active life Dr. L. and his medicine enable me to have. Many days the pain is very bad, especially in my feet, hands, and wrists, but as always, I take the smallest dose I can to function normally and stay on the lookout for any other cures.

Life rolls on—its great engine ceaselessly churning out memories, friendship, heartache, setbacks, growth, and triumph—all those things that make normal life worth all the effort.

March–December. Elaine enters the same school Eugene is leaving. We give him a trip to Europe for graduation. Wei's architecture business booms. His model for the Chinatown Housing and Elementary School makes the newspapers. We buy a Dodge Charger for $4,000. Eugene gets a job delivering dry cleaning and his first summer paycheck: $52.50.

I sell insurance, I get the apartment ready for painting, and I have cramps in my abdomen so excruciating that I want to die. Even though I'm used to pain, this is something else. Hospital, surgery, hysterectomy: just three words. Recovering from it: three lifetimes.

However, because of how healthy I keep myself to fight my RA, my recovery is impressively quick. The doctor is amazed. Eugene comes home from college for Thanksgiving and Christmas. On New Year's Eve, Elaine is able to stay up with us and watch the crystal ball descend in Times Square for the first time in her life. The look in her eyes and her little body next to mine were worth every agony of the year.

1970. My hands and feet really hurt, especially in the morning and especially when it snows. It seems to take a week of effort just to start a day, but I don't want to give up. *Mother, give me courage; Father, give me will; God, give me strength.*

I make myself take up my insurance work again for the first time in months. We put on dinner parties. We go to dinner parties. Eugene joins a band at school, gets good grades, and starts a summer job at HIP. They think he's some kind of genius. I teach Elaine a few Chinese words a day.

We spend the summer in New Hampshire. The mountain air fills me like a healing spirit. In all of nature, mountains are my greatest love. When I was a child, our family spent summers in the great mountains of China, and I recall the long trip in sedan chairs from the port on the Yangtze. Breathing the clean air of the New England countryside, I can still hear the "hee-ho, hee-ho" of the carriers. With this rhythmic chant, my family was carried up the mountain to our house. With so many in the family—as well as the chef and the maids—the procession was very long and beautiful.

Back in the city, hay fever lays me low again—Elaine too, though she can sleep. I can't. I'm so tired of this! Lying in such discomfort in a comfortable bed staring wide-eyed at another long night of misery—I want to scream, but I don't want to wake anybody. But here's Wei, rustling next to me, his caring eyes and playful smile making the darkness friendlier, gently taking my hand, soothing my brow like I'm a priceless treasure, keeping me company through the night. No wonder I won't give up.

My allergies are so severe this time that we go live for a while in the central air-conditioning at my sister's in Michigan, where Eugene is starting his sophomore year. This helps relieve the headaches, fatigue, dizziness, and choking feeling—as does the Benadryl her doctor friend suggests.

Back home, an electric air cleaner is put in my room, and I start going to sales meetings again. An allergist pokes me with needles and declares that something I breathe is the culprit. He puts me on Actifed, which I take at night. It works! Ahh.

My RA continues with its ups and downs, just like my life. My heart fills as Elaine takes a public bus to school for the first time and breaks when I hear my sixth brother has died.

1971–1972. I am relentless in my search for relief from rheumatoid arthritis. I see a Chinese herbalist. "Twenty years you've had this," he says. "Not much I can do." He prescribes some herbs to boil for soaking and washing my deforming hands and feet. They seem to help.

I start reading books about health and health food as intensely as my father used to pore over the stock market. I go to the health food center for natural foods and vitamins. I learn on my own what helps my condition.

Two of my sisters also have RA (a strong indication that it's inherited). I pass what I learn on to them. They report that it's helping them, particularly the vitamins. This encourages me to further pursue the self-care route. Acidic foods and sugar, I learn, can make my joint pain acute. Abstaining from these foods lessens the number and sharpness of RA flare-ups.

I have a football-sized ovarian cyst removed. The good news is they found no cancer, and they took out my appendix too, and many visitors come and comfort me. The bad news is the terrible pain I have in my shoulder when I come out of the anesthesia. I had been lying on my side for twenty-four hours, inflaming my RA mercilessly. As soon as I can eat solids again, I start back on my vitamins. The relief the vitamins gives my pain is undeniable. From here on, I believe in food supplements all the way.

The search for health continues. I cut back more on gas-producing foods to cut out the feeling of being bloated. I wean myself from Actifed and get more outlets in our apartment for more allergy-fighting AC units. I start trudging to Chinatown for acupuncture from Dr. Lee, who becomes my friend. Right away we like each other and strike up a bargain. I teach her some English, and she charges me less.

She pinpoints twenty-four needles in my legs and feet, hands and wrists, and the right side of my neck. I lie there an hour as my circulation alters favorably—twice a week, always temporary relief at the beginning. But over time, enduring improvement.

I continue to take Dr. L.'s elixir as little as possible to function. I am so grateful to him for the strength to pursue further improvements for my RA. On one trip to see him, Elaine is with me, and I like that she likes him too.

However, the year ends sadly with the news of Dr. L.'s death, and then President Truman's. I pray my thanks for the lives of these decent, great men.

CHAPTER 5

NORMAL LIFE WITH RA

1973. When rheumatoid arthritis first struck me twenty-three years ago, all my plans were shattered. My new world of pain sometimes made it impossible to see even one moment into the future. Sometimes I lay in bed agonizing over whether to move my head just one half-inch to the left, for sometimes even a tiny movement could cause hours of greater pain. Through the fog and fire of this terrible new war in my body, a new goal for the future gradually emerged, a new dream that nothing could shatter: *to live a normal life with my RA.*

Now who's normal? No one is, really. It's not the first word I'd use to describe myself! You could even say it's normal to be abnormal. Each of us is special and has a unique life story, but you know what I mean. On the other hand, most people have many things in common: things that make up what we call normal life. There's family with its joys and heartaches—births, deaths, sickness, separation, children, school, weddings, divorces, laughing, sobbing, the house, the car, the cleaning, the plumbing, the decorating, the holidays, the Thursdays, the leaving home, the letters home, the e-mail, and all the rest. And our work, the office, the clients, the customers, the people we work with, the job well-done, the screw-ups, the crushing deadlines, our tools (pen, phone, vehicle, computer, envelopes, machine press, whatever it may be). Then, of course, there are our friends and neighbors and the world we live in: saying hi, playing cards, dancing, dealing with horrible weather, enjoying mountain air, voting, reading the paper, yelling at the politicians on the TV screen, and so on.

The world of normal life is extraordinarily rich and unique for all, as well as comfortingly familiar. Sometimes it seems so normal we hardly take time to notice or appreciate it. We take it for granted until it's taken from us. Then we long for it like we long for air. That's how I longed for it, and I left no stone unturned working for it. As much as my story is one of overcoming RA, it is also one of finding a way to enjoy normal life.

By 1973, I have finally achieved what you could call a normal life, thanks to Dr. L.'s medicine and my own research into diet and vitamins—plus regular exercise and acupuncture. However, normal life with RA is different than normal life. It's accompanied by the guest who refuses to leave: pain. Sometimes this obnoxious guest shouts so loudly that you can barely hear your own thoughts, let alone what others are saying. But with a minimum amount of medicine, good diet, and the rest, I'm now able to muffle RA's voice and restrain its thrashing enough to hear and enjoy the normal life God has granted me. Moreover, I never take it for granted any more.

Normal life! Here I am, right in the thick of it. Cooking, cleaning, ironing, laundry, sewing, knitting, driving—I like it so much; my hands are always busy. However, my hands are RA's favorite places, so normal life costs me.

Imagine having to pay for the privilege of ironing and folding clothes! Nevertheless, that's how it is for folks with RA. I have some elderly friends I help when they need me. I have what you might call an advanced understanding of the aches and pains in their aging bodies. I stand at my business meetings and speak of insurance as my ankles and feet quietly sing, feeling like I'm standing on poisoned pins and needles. My son calls from college, excited about his architecture plans. I don't miss a word as I shift the phone ten times or more to keep my shoulder from making me faint. Normal life! Believe it or not, I thank God for every second of it.

April. It's such an uplifting experience to find a spiritual guide, someone who cuts through the clutter in your mind and puts lightness in your heart, an expansive feeling that lasts throughout the week. I hope everyone with RA (or even without it) finds this kind of guidance. I can't imagine how to endure the cross of this disease without a guide. The spiritual is not just part of normal life for me; it's the *heart* of it—the burning bush, so to speak—that ultimately consumes all hellish pain. I have found my guide: the Reverend Schuller and his *Hour of Power* on TV. His service always has such a positive effect on me! I really like him. His call for "possibility thinking" constantly encourages me. Watching his show every Sunday is now the foundation of my normal life.

Summer. Vacation travels are meant to be fun, but can they be with feet like mine? Yes, if the walking is scheduled between good rest and recovery time—in addition, of course, to my own attention to health and possibility thinking. In Europe and New Hampshire, we have quite a time. Just like normal folk!

Autumn. Eugene tells us he's taking a year off from school to do architectural rendering. He's always a considerate son, and we try to stay open to his choices, but it's a difficult thing to accept. Life is what happens when you expect something else! My usual fall hay fever diverts me from worrying about this too much, and so does my subsequent flaring arthritis. Strange helpers!

Wei breaks ground for his front-page project: Confucius Plaza, the first housing and school project in Chinatown. But there are ominous rumblings between him and his business partner, who is bringing his marital problems to work. Ups and downs may be part of normal life, but, oh Lord, how deeply they affect us. This particular stress threatens my RA dangerously. Prayer and more diet research help me maintain. I work on cutting out all refined sugar and bad carbohydrates and continue acupuncture.

Winter. Eugene can't come home for the holidays but has a friend hand-deliver his beautiful presents. Our son's thoughtfulness is a Christmas present we receive all year round. Then our twenty-fifth wedding anniversary is spent with our attorney, hashing out problems with Wei's business partner. This gets me feeling low, so I make a hot pot.

I often make hot pots for my friends and family. Are you familiar with this Chinese treat? My version of the hot pot starts with a fresh broth made from a whole chicken. Then I put the broth in the stainless steel chafing dish with Sterno fire underneath and place the chafing dish on the center of the dining table. In the broth, I add some raw foods, vegetables, and whatever each one fancies to be cooked in the chafing dish. That is the fun of having the hot pot with family sitting around the table. The delicious foods are cooked right in front of us and each one can dish out the foods he or she likes in the bowl and enjoy it piping hot. Some foods, such as shrimp balls and meatballs, are half-cooked, steamed, or fried. I use ground turkey for meatballs now. A hot pot calls for a good bit of work, with the slicing and dicing. My RA affects me when I make it! Nevertheless, it's very delicious and adds the perfect warmth to our quiet New Year's Eve. Thank you, Lord, for this peace in the storm, and for helping me cut back on the medicine I take.

1974. My happy, busy, painful life rolls on in the unique way I call normal: up and down and sideways! Long gas lines, a vacation that flies at the speed of light, and constant wrangling with Wei's partner. This gets so overwhelming, sometimes Wei and I just hold hands and pray, and a wonderful miracle happens: Life goes on! *Hour of Power,* acupuncture, reduced medicine, and improved health!

I try a seven-day diet from a book that claims to cure arthritis. One day of fasting—not even taking my medicine. Next day: the book diet, three aspirin, and a scalding, skin-cleansing bath. The third day I have a banana, and the fourth day I have had enough! I go back to my normal regime.

1975. Wei and his partner officially call it quits, and I work in Wei's office to take up the slack. Wei does the architecture, and I get to do all the job estimates, bookkeeping, writing of paychecks, and what seems to be endless et ceteras!

Moreover, Elaine now has braces, so we have to economize. I again do all our housework myself. My RA has a field day with this kind of schedule, and I do what I can to get by. I eliminate red meat from my diet and ration my medicine and acupuncture. Some days I feel super, and some days I couldn't feel more mortal.

I still sew a lot, especially for my darling Elaine. However, allergy season again tips the tide, and I can't sleep from the headaches and the choking feeling. This is the time when Wei's mother decides to thank me for the lamb shank I bring her and her husband by saying, "If you have time to cook, why don't you help Wei in his office?" When she finds out I have been helping Wei there, she says all I do is have coffee and talk on the phone. I don't even drink coffee! Wei's sister tells me it's just her mother's unstable mind and not to take her seriously. I know this makes sense, but the extra stress she causes *is* serious.

My primary doctor discovers I have hypothyroidism, which explains my dizziness, headaches, and listless feeling. He advises taking it easy for a while and sends me to a new rheumatologist.

Dr. C. finds my sedimentation count unusually high and puts me on prednisone alone (without Dr. L.'s added hormones) and doses of Synthroid and Plaquenil.

Wei has good news about his office. He has a number of new architectural projects so that he can hire more employees. I thank God I can ease off some there. Eugene gives us a precious week visit for Christmas, and by year's end my various conditions are heading toward tolerably normal again.

1976. I begin America's bicentennial year with a diet from a book by Dr. S. in San Francisco. I don't follow his thirty-day program exactly, but I don't eat his "don't" foods, and I do eat just his "do" foods.

Dr. S.'s Soup

In a blender, put 1 cup of cooked rice, 1 cup of sliced vegetables (such as carrots, onions, or broccoli), 3 ounces of tuna or diced chicken breast, 2 cups of water, and a dash of salt. Blend thoroughly. Add another cup of water. Pour the mixture into a pot and heat until boiling. Mix in a tablespoon of safflower oil or canola oil. Pour the soup into a thermos bottle for drinking throughout the day.

When Dr. S. has a very hectic schedule and cannot have regular meals, he drinks one cup of his soup every two hours to keep nourished.

Nevertheless, I'm still getting headaches, and I'm dizzy, so I ask Dr. C. for a natural thyroid medicine. He gives me Armour tablets, which are better, but in February, I quit Dr. C. and go back to Dr. L.'s medicine.

I go to San Francisco and meet Dr. S., who gives me acupuncture and vitamin injections (B6 and B12) right into my swollen joints. These are so painful I grit my teeth, but after a number of his treatments, the swelling goes down. I also try a new pain reliever he prescribes, Darvon (65 mg), and his special soup (chicken or tuna, rice, and veggies—all blended, then heated with safflower oil, one cup every two hours). Moreover, it's great being with Elaine in San Francisco and seeing her godparents, who are my sister and her husband.

By autumn, I'm feeling well again with no more headaches or dizziness. I'm able to help Wei at work again, and I reduce Dr. L.'s medicine more and more, until I try taking none at all. Before long, a painful flare-up begins, and I resume taking the medication in small amounts.

Things get more or less normal again, and the winter holidays are fun.

1977, March. Death, we're told, is part of normal life. However, this is great grief when it happens close to home. One of my dearest brothers has died young of a heart attack. My heart is breaking.

July–August. We spend our summer in New Hampshire. My health and arthritis are better as long as I adhere to my diet. I'm also able to continue conducting my business over the phone, which is a great boon.

December. My unmarried brother goes into the emergency room for surgery. Dear God, not him too!

His operation goes well. He has a bleeding ulcer like our father's. We take him in to help him recuperate. Merciful Lord, thank you.

1978. My brother recovers and returns to his own place. My RA is getting more manageable, and reducing my medicine slims me. People say I look younger, too. For that I thank diet and exercise.

Teeth! Ah yes. Seeing the dentist. This is how most people normally learn about serious pain. This summer in New Hampshire, I have excruciating pain in my two right molars. The local dentist can't help me out. I have to drive back and forth between two New Hampshire towns—sixty miles with Elaine by my side—to have these two teeth extracted. It is very hard, even for a tough, pain-trained RA pro like me. I'm just glad I wasn't born before Novocain was created.

There are also big changes in normal life. I resign from mutual funds and stay with insurance, freeing more time to help Wei out. Wei gets a perfect new office—smaller but sunnier—on the top floor of a Fifth Avenue building. My primary doctor retires early because his wife dies. It's very sad. I will miss him. He's a good man: my commander-in-chief through my wars with RA. Eugene comes home for the holidays with lovely Mia. They tell us they're engaged!

How can time move this fast? My heart is pounding! I make a hot pot! Happy New Year!

1979. The routine months melt away like ice in the Sun. My RA adds its usual dramatic flourishes, fluctuating drastically as it so often does. Some days are pure hell, others just slight purgatory. I vary my medicine intake, trying to catch up with the pain, but this doesn't work all the time. Through it all, normal life rolls on magnificently: sometimes a big river, sometimes a mountain stream.

Elaine and I like our new doctor, Dr. D. Our New Hampshire vacation gives us lots of lobster and mountain air. I even play a little Frisbee. I'm not bad for a long-time RA gal—I'm nimble!

Then, ah! *August 17, Michigan:* Eugene and Mia's wedding! Elaine wears the bridesmaid gown I sewed for her, and, of course, she looks beautiful. Over two hundred people celebrate with us, and the whole event is as artful and wonderful as the bride and groom themselves. It's one of the happiest days in my life.

Around Thanksgiving, we give Eugene and Mia a reception for our New York group of people. Mia and our family and friends finally meet here, and it all goes well. Mia's mother and grandmother fly in for the occasion and get quite a kick out of New York City and its colorful characters!

It is time for the apartment to be painted. I can't keep from working like a mad woman when this happens. I guess it's just my nature—I smell the paint, and I can't stop till all the shelves are cleared! My feet burn from the pain, even with my well-padded (and expensive!) orthopedic shoes. Oh well, the new paint makes the apartment look so fresh and bright!

This is exactly the same way I feel now about my normal life. (Quiet prayer of thanks.)

CHAPTER 6

MAJOR EVENTS, RUNNING THEMES, AND MY GROWING BODY OF RESEARCH

1980. Looking over my life, as I have done with my diaries, I begin to see patterns that make the story *my* story. Sure, I come across many things I thought were significant then, but now make me wonder, "Why did I even write that down?" However, the big events stand out, the milestones, weddings, and bouts of serious illness, things like that.

In addition, patterns emerge that I didn't realize were patterns when I was living them. Like my hot pot for New Year's, both Chinese and American, and how I test my physical health every few years by cleaning all our blinds in the bathtub. Like my knitting, my piano playing, my prayer life, and my never-ending research into how to live thankfully with rheumatoid arthritis.

Many themes emerge during these years. One of the biggest themes is the headache of clearing up the accounting caused by Wei dissolving his partnership. We finally have to file for arbitration. This blasted thing will drag on a dozen years—four more years to go!

Another recurring theme is my seasonal allergies. They regularly rob my sleep and get my RA all worked up. However, this year my growing body of research into diet greatly lessens hay fever's hold on me.

Acupuncture is another strong thread in the tapestry of my life. It always helps me, and its cumulative effect over time just can't be denied. I used to have it done almost forty times a year, now it's less than twenty.

And helping Wei in his office—that's major. It seems now I do almost everything but the architecture! The huge amount of typing takes its toll on my poor hands, but what can you do? Hard work is hard on anybody—we all know that, but the consultants like that I'm so reliable. I always pay them their fees on time! (This is very important.)

Then there're the little moments in our lives that end up being major events in disguise. Some magic happens in these moments that stretches through all the years and touches other moments. The beautiful American woman showing me the few grains of rice at the bottom of the orphanage food barrel was one such moment.

Another occurs this summer when Wei and I drop into a Dunkin' Donuts for a vacation snack. Six ten-year-olds bustle in and ask for water. The kind waitress serves them graciously. Moreover, Wei and I offer and treat each of them to a donut. This little gesture makes them so happy! Their smiling faces make our day, and many years in the future something happens that puts those very same smiles on our own faces. (I'll tell you later.)

1981. My dear Elaine! She is such a blessing to me! As I've said before, the best decision I ever made was to have her. It was so good of my doctor to tell me when I was thirty-seven that my health had improved enough to have another child. Yes, it was a long, hard decision—nothing I could take lightly in any way. Nevertheless, thank holy wisdom herself—she who is the female side of God—for guiding my decision to say *yes!* Life without Elaine would not be life at all for me. As I've said, she was born with the face I prayed to see.

Of course, I love my son just as much, but now I am feeling the great strength of my connection with my daughter because now we both are women. Going with Elaine to look at colleges last year stirred profound feelings within me. The big event of her leaving our nest and going to college loomed so large and soon in our future! Now, she's a vision in the long Chantilly lace Chinese gown she wears for graduation. She's won the esteemed Beneficial-Hodson Scholarship (based solely on scholastic achievement) to Johns Hopkins University. We are so proud of her.

She's going away from home so soon, and our remaining time races by. One moment she's taking driving lessons, the next we're doing jigsaw puzzles in New Hampshire on summer vacation, and suddenly we're driving her to her dorm room in Baltimore. (I'm glad it's driving distance from New York, at least.)

We buy her a little refrigerator for her freshman dorm room. Little do I suspect how much I'll be stocking that little fridge for the next year (and all her fridges through college—another running theme). We also buy her a little window fan. We've done all we can to make her new life comfortable. We wave good-bye. Good-bye, beautiful one, my best companion, my helper, Elaine—you—good-bye.

You know the story. We talk on the phone. She's homesick, and I'm sorry (but secretly happy a little), and the food there is terrible! I think two things at the same time: *How can they expect their students to learn without good nutrition?* And: *Oh good, I can still cook for her!*

Right away, I mix up a batch of deliciously good stuff for her. A reason to visit! We come bearing food, rugs, and a bedspread and there she is again! It's amazing how it soothes me just to see her in the flesh. She's tired-looking and thin, but getting straight As (and perfect scores in calculus). Her face relaxes when she sees all the food we crunch into that wonderful midget appliance it was so smart of us to buy.

Running themes, major events. *The New York Times* runs an article and drawing of another housing project that Wei designed. Eugene takes two eight-hour exams to become a registered architect like his father, and Elaine comes home for Christmas! We both suffer from miserable tooth pain, but I thank God anyway. (We always did like doing things together.)

1982! Eugene gets his architect's license—like father, like son! In addition, we finally win the arbitration suit against Wei's crazy partner! Free at last (except we have to wait two more years before the check finally arrives), and I fill Elaine's refrigerator lots and lots of times and get her a typewriter and a table.

Then (drumroll, please) comes the big event of this period, perhaps the culmination of all these little triumphs of normal life. On a beautiful spring morning in early May—May 2 to be exact—*Wei and I walk forty blocks on Broadway—two miles!—and my feet and legs don't complain one bit!* (Bring in the trumpets and fanfare.)

Any of you out there who have RA understand how momentous this is. To do it just once in the middle of a pain-filled life is like winning an Olympic gold medal. What Olympic winner doesn't remember the glory of that golden day? They remember all the training and the sacrifice and the pains they endured to achieve it. I remember all that too—and all the trial-and-error research I did and my determination never to back down from this bullying disease. My gold medal may not be visible, but it's always there for me, a solid and solemn reminder: *You are a victor over, not a victim of, rheumatoid arthritis.*

1983–1987. Of course, I'm not through with pains in my joints after walking or working with my hands. There is no cure for RA. No one knows that in his or her bones more than I do, but I'm happy that I can hike pain-free a little more frequently, like on vacation in the hills of New Hampshire or on travels abroad with Elaine.

My condition improves more than it declines due to my gathering knowledge of diet and supplements. Alfalfa tablets, garlic, fish oil—and all the things I list in the self-help chapter of this book—are the best weapons I (or anyone) have found in the battle against RA. I start to get more and more responses from friends and acquaintances asking and thanking me for my advice in these matters. I'm always more than glad to help, and writing this book is just one more way of distributing this knowledge. Even to this day, I'm still reading, researching, and discovering new ways of relieving RA. Most everything I find also gives comfort to regular arthritis victims.

During this period, Elaine goes through college and graduates Phi Beta Kappa with a prestigious physics award. My heart swells when she gets a full tuition grant for graduate work at my father's alma mater, the University of Chicago. How the wheel of time turns round!

We give her a European tour for her graduation, and I'm thrilled I can join her for most of it. What better reward could there be for all my efforts in fighting my disease?

We see England: the Tower of London, Westminster Abbey, and Big Ben.

Then we travel the rolling hills of Wales. There we have honey rose petal ice cream and sway to the hypnotic Welsh singers singing their hearts out for us.

There're many poor people here, but it's very safe. We come upon a Chinese takeout place and drop in to have a chat. The whole wall's a menu, and a customer there empties his pockets of change and asks the owner how much that will buy. He's so happy to hear us address him in Chinese and gets very excited when we say where we're from. "Will you talk to my wife on the phone?" he asks us. He's called her to ask what to order. I talk with his wife, and she's more excited than her husband—New York to her is the end of the rainbow! Elaine and I are very glad we dropped in this Welsh Chinese restaurant, owned by a man from Liverpool!

We return to England and do (among many other things) the Wax Museum (OK, but they looked so lifeless!), Harrods' famous food emporium (disappointing—Heinz ketchup is a specialty?), and Buckingham Palace (we were lucky to see the royal band practice). Finally, we take the eight-hour trip from London back to New York and into Wei's happy arms at the airport.

All of you with RA, remember: *Who says you can't see the world?*

Wei Foo, Eugene, and I help Elaine move truckloads of stuff (*how did she fit all this into that little apartment she had?*) into her new Windy City place. Eugene—who now has a black belt in karate—is such a good brother to Elaine. It pleases Wei and me so much to see how they get along. Meanwhile, I say hello to the regular-size fridge she has there. My days of putting lots of tasty good food into Elaine's refrigerator are very far from over, but it's OK by me.

They find a tumor in Wei's father's lung. He has always been fond of me, despite his mean-spirited wife, who is anything but. I like him right back. He's usually very jolly, but now it's so sad—things are getting grave. His condition goes downhill fast, and the doctors can't discharge him from the hospital.

Wei is very down, and I'm more than glad to let him lean on me. After all, he's always offered me all the kindness and support any woman could ask for.

After a nightmarish month of tests and no-win decisions, the doctors realize they can't do anything for Wei's father except make him comfortable with morphine.

With just a day or two left to live, this wonderful man takes off his oxygen mask, speaks directly to me about his funeral, and requests I handle the arrangements. He is lucid enough to know exactly who is good at what.

I arrange for him to be baptized and given last rites, and one of his last gestures is to shake my hand in thanks and say good-bye. When he dies, Wei and I are the only family in the room to send him off. Wei's mother takes the news surprisingly well, while one loudmouth member of Wei's family predictably opposes every suggestion anyone makes about the obituary and other matters. There's always someone like that at family occasions, it seems.

I take care of all the funeral arrangements, just as I promised, and that part goes well at least. A huge number of people come, and many beautiful flowers offer their quiet respects to this friendly man who liked people so much.

Wei and I quietly carry sadness around for quite a while after this. Work is piling up at the office, however, and soon we get right back to it.

As Reverend Schuller says, with every death there's birth. Eugene's wife, Mia, brings our first grandchild into the world in Michigan: Tarryn. She's so unbelievably beautiful.

Time rushes by like a happy child running from room to room. Tarryn turns over by herself. Tarryn sits up! On the phone I hear that she's crawling. One Christmas I see her stand by herself. The next Christmas, she's walking and talking, sharp as a blade!

The best part is that she warms to me like we're long-lost friends. We play for an hour while her mother rests, and she talks nonstop. And such a vocabulary! How does a two-and-a-half-year-old learn words like *absolutely* and *extraordinary*? Elaine was like that, too.

Then, even more life. Tarryn gets a little sister, Alyson. Perhaps it won't surprise you to learn that I think she's extra beautiful too!

I'm taking only a small dose of medicine now and get acupuncture less than five times a year. I'm still actively researching diet and ways to good health and less pain from arthritis. I even try green-lipped mussel capsules. I hear it helps some arthritics, but I'm not one of the lucky ones. I have to stop it soon because it seems to make things worse rather than better. Oh well, no real harm in trying.

Life is amazing. One day I write in my diary that I feel very, very well, and I'm seldom tired. Less than two months later, my brother has cancer surgery and a bad prognosis, and I write in my diary: "I have been a positive person all my life, but there are still times—the work, my arthritis, and crises in the family get me down. I begin to feel like a deflated balloon. Just hope this feeling will go away. This is not me."

Up and down, life goes on. I have the piano tuned so I can play carols at Christmas. We celebrate our thirty-seventh wedding anniversary—I can't believe it's been that long. The children and grandchildren visit and give us true holiday cheer. A few months later, in my annual physical, Dr. D finds a lump in my left breast.

CHAPTER 7

AGING IS NOT FOR THE FAINTHEARTED

1987, March. The breast surgeon says my X-rays show a big patch on my left breast with star-ray spikes coming out on one side and a small dot on my right breast. The chances for malignancy are fifty-fifty. I arrange with my good friend and neighbor to help Wei in the office, and I enter the hospital.

Blood tests, EKG, X-rays, mammograms—a doctor studies my X-rays to measure where the dot in my right breast is. She gives me a painful local anesthetic. My veins are very fine, and she punctures one. She tries again, probing the needle toward the dot, then more X-rays. The doctor is still off-target. She pulls out the needle and tries a different spot. More X-rays. Bull's-eye. She puts a fine wire in the hollow needle that curls like a hook in front, very delicate, very intricate. I'm wheeled to the OR. The anesthesiologist is a Chinese woman. We converse in Mandarin, and then I'm dead to the world.

I come to. I touch my side and find my breast still there. Just to make sure, I peep into my dressing gown and see them both intact. I'm so happy.

However, my happiness soon turns to concern again when the pathologist says he needs more time with the biopsy.

The next morning, I have the mastectomy of the left breast, as I had previously consented. The tumor is minuscule, but deadly nonetheless. In recovery, propped up in bed, I feel quite well. When Wei comes to see me later in the day, he tells me that I look so good he wondered if I had the surgery.

While I'm in the hospital, I'm shocked to hear from my San Francisco sister that her husband has died of a heart attack. He was very dear to me, and I'm sad I can't be at his funeral. His goddaughter, my Elaine, goes for us all.

The doctors say I'm healing very fast, and I'm discharged a week after surgery. Even though I'm sixty-two, my attention to healthy diet pays off in spades when I need to heal.

I have to stop Dr. L.'s medicine (after twenty-four years) because it contains estrogen. I start with iron and a high dose of plain prednisone, 17.5 mg daily.

April. My sister-in-law calls. "Wei's mother is in tears about your misfortune," she says. "She wants me to take her to visit you, but I can't manage driving her by myself and helping her get around, especially because she's so superstitious about hospitals, and they depress her so much." I appreciate this about-face in my mother-in-law, and I'm happy she finally understands what kind of person I am. It's rather late in the game, but still—I thank God for paving the way.

I get my stitches out, and the surgeon gives me the good news: my right breast has no cancer, just a little calcification called an intraductal papilloma. The left breast had the cancer called lobular carcinoma, but my lymph is clear of cancer. Once again I thank the Lord.

You know me. I try to reduce my medicine to as much as I can to get along. For the rest of the month, I gradually taper my prednisone from 17.5 mg a day to 10 mg with two Bufferins. I start doing office work in the evening at home, and before long I'm going to the office again.

May–December. It's a good thing I heal quickly. This business of getting older calls for toughness and strength—pressing family business calls from Taiwan. Visas, travel arrangements, phone calls, all this sort of thing. Two months after major surgery, I arrive in Taipei with my two sisters.

Discussions, decisions, exhausting family dynamics—two weeks pass, and I fly home again, a twelve-hour trip. I start organizing my high school reunion and go to Washington DC to interview our guest speaker, Nien Cheng, author of *Life and Death in Shanghai.* She's a wonderful woman and a true inspiration. What horrors she's seen and experienced during the awful fall of Shanghai, the same debacle my parents had to escape. Furthermore, she writes so well and remains such a pure soul despite the evil that's visited her life. I am so lucky to have met her and have her speak for our reunion.

Then it's back home to visit children, work in the office, and have the reunion. It's a great success, and I breathe a huge sigh of relief with the pleasure of a job well-done.

Wei and I start getting hour-long massages every Sunday. This helps very much. I add a new Chinese herb for arthritis to my daily regime and cut out sugar.

I have a brilliant idea, and I get my two sisters to come see me in New York to celebrate their seventieth and sixtieth birthdays. We have a great ten days together with dinner and theater and much laughter and conversation. My heart is further refreshed when high-spirited little Tarryn leads everyone in singing "Happy Birthday" to me on my sixty-third birthday and when Elaine decorates our Christmas tree as she always does.

A lot happened this year, Lord. It's all life, and I thank you for your mercies.

1988. My brother B. is dying in Taiwan. He says I'm the only sibling that cares, and I'm both his sister and friend. I get chills and fever on the twenty-hour journey Wei and I make to see him.

There are more family discussions, decisions, attorneys, and B.'s manic-depressive wife in her manic stage. B. is dying of cancer and internal bleeding. It's hard for me to stay tough, but there's too much to do for me to be weak. We fly back to New York and buy glass niches in the New York cemetery for B. and his wife. We keep in touch with how B. is doing, and in about a month we hear the ammonia in his blood is reaching mortal limits.

My trusty travel companion, Elaine, goes with me this time. B. is happy to see me. He's at the end of his journey, but his eyes still have energy. He's been a nonbeliever all his life, but now he asks me to arrange for baptism and last rites. Happily, there's time to get him what he wants.

Then, sadly, he passes on. I feel so much grief that I can hardly think.

I get a bright red silk bag with a drawstring made to line his urn. I do so to honor my brother, who was very neat and tidy in every detail. His wife, blessedly, is in the quiet stage of her neurosis, so there's a peaceful air to all the business, and we can take her to a doctor for medication. Elaine and I fly the urn back to New York for interment. I gain five pounds from two weeks of unhealthy Taiwanese food.

Time to live. December in Hawaii with friends: muumuus, hulas, luaus, beaches, canoeing, dancing, more dancing, shopping, and the Dole cannery! That should do it. Back home to work, and a mountain of mail and weeks of preparing a big celebration for our fortieth anniversary greet us.

And it is a celebration. Even Wei's mother has a great time!

Thank you, Lord, for life: hard, easy, and in-between!

CHAPTER 8

AND THE CROOKED SHALL BE MADE STRAIGHT

1989. In this period of my life, I get into surgeries to fix the deformities from my RA. I continue with acupuncture and massage and begin to explore new healing techniques and diet supplements such as herbal pills and primrose.

I even try Dr. K.'s unusual but interesting energy treatment.

Dr. K. has me lie down on a cot, then he talks to me a little. Then, without touching—or only light touching—he moves his hands all over me from head to toe. I can feel the heat and vibrations from his hands even though they're an inch away. Then I sit up, and he does the same thing. I still feel pulsing vibes from his hands even though they don't shake at all. The next day I feel light and quite free of pain, and I'm hoping the treatment will miraculously heal me. I have about twenty sessions in four months, and I stop. The effect wears off, and lately I'm seeing no improvement.

I turn to an orthopedic surgeon. Hope springs eternal. Modern medicine is miracle enough for me. I'd just like to start the new decade with a new pair of feet! The surgeon tells me she's had cases of deformity just as severe as mine, and her success rate is 95 percent. I schedule two surgeries for January and March.

1990, January 17. The day I get pretested for my right foot surgery, our first grandson is born: Anthony! There ought to be a proverb: a handsome child is a very auspicious sign.

January–March. Hospitals—even though I'm becoming a pro at being a hospital patient, there are still things no one can do much about. My roommate either snores or has her TV blasting until midnight. Then she calls for the nurse half a dozen times and shuffles around on her inflatable mattress like a big fish making sha-sha-sha sounds through the rest of the night.

I have my two-hour surgery with a local anesthesia, which I prefer if I can get it.

My new roommate's a talker, yakking nonstop, so I ask to be discharged. I wait half an hour for a wheelchair, and then an aide wheels me to the emergency room. She asks me to get out and sit while I wait for Wei to get a taxi and tells me I can then walk down a forty-foot exit ramp outside. I've just had foot surgery, and she wants me to take a little stroll!

I tell her I'm under doctor's orders not to walk. No, she insists, she has to go right away and needs the wheelchair. I offer a compromise: wheel me down the ramp, and I'll wait on one foot like a stork for Wei to fetch me. No, no, she says, she can't take that responsibility, and besides, she doesn't have her coat and might catch cold.

No arguing with this one. I just sit there in the wheelchair. She keeps saying she has to go. I keep sitting. By now the whole waiting room is laughing. Finally, Wei and a kind security guard push me down the ramp.

A long letter was written to the administrator. I receive a phone call with profuse apologies, explaining that the aide was new and didn't know any better. Hospitals! I'm glad anyway; I was able to entertain the people in the waiting room.

After a week at home, taking it easy with my foot elevated, I slowly feel like myself again and start making calls and writing letters. My foot swells and the skin turns red, but the surgeon said this happens with patients on prednisone. She prescribes the antibiotic Cipro and that clears up the problem nicely. In addition, the X-rays show my toes are all straight now! I heal quickly as usual, and before long I can walk to the hairdresser's and I can use my Exercycle again (on good days).

I have to be careful, though, to make sure I keep my foot elevated enough each day. Sometimes, like when we visit adorable Anthony and have busy family gatherings, I don't elevate it enough, and it swells. There's some recurring infection then too, but Cipro takes care of it.

April–June. Wei's mother is ninety-five when she dies. The nurse who took care of her confides that she was very difficult. This is no surprise!

She was my mother-in-law for exactly forty-one years, three months, and one week. This is a long, hard, heavy book to finally close. May the poor, lonely woman find good company now—wherever she's going.

The doctor takes the first pin out of my toes. The "pin" is actually a three-inch screw. I bleed for a few hours. In two days, I'm back in Wei's office doing tax returns. In two more weeks, out comes the second screw. I need more recuperative rest than I had figured. Then I get an ingrown toenail infection. There's always something! Cipro takes care of it.

By April, I'm wearing my own shoe again (one-inch heel), and in May, I'm back in the office on my regular schedule again.

July. Alaska on Princess Cruises! The mountains and glaciers! The aroma of fresh salmon over open charcoal pits! I've never tasted such salmon. I wonder what spices they use. On the ship there is a special dinner to celebrate the twenty-fifth anniversary of Princess Cruises. When it is time for dessert, all the lights are turned off in the dining room and lively music is turned on. The waiters march out to the beat of the music holding trays of baked Alaska above their heads with their right hands and keeping their left hands behind their backs. The room is lit only by the candles that are burning on top of the baked Alaska. The flickering of all the flames makes the occasion breathtaking. The waiters look handsome in their elegant red and black uniforms. What a grand spectacle! When the last waiter arrives at his designated table, the room lights are turned back on and the passengers applaud loudly. The baked Alaska looks too beautiful to eat—but it is absolutely delicious. What a magnificent trip! I gain almost four pounds, but I'll happily work it off.

August. The doctor finds my right foot is doing well, and I schedule work on my left for October. I have a few days now when I feel so good; there's almost no pain.

Our masseuse brings me a miracle lamp from China. It has a perforated metal plate with over thirty minerals in it, and no bulbs—good for all aches and pains. I start using it on my swollen right knee. It helps some.

October. I catch a virus, and my right knee and elbow flare up badly. Whenever I get a cold, my joints give me trouble.

My dear older sister has a stroke. My other Taiwan brother dies of a heart attack. I go into the hospital for surgery with a heavy heart, full of prayers for my family.

After the usual hospital nonsense—long waits for nothing, being nudged awake from deep sleep to take a sleeping pill—I have surgery on my left foot and a minor adjustment to the right. Three days later, I'm discharged—after waiting a half hour in a wheelchair, of course.

My sister is improving and can swallow a little now. She moves to a rehab center.

My follow-up X-rays show that the surgery was a success. The doctor only puts one pin in this time, and when pus forms around it, she takes it out earlier than intended. All's well, though, that ends well.

I'm able to end the year visiting my sister in Michigan. It's sad to see her so frail, but we both feel it's a blessing to be with each other.

1991. Slowly but surely, I reduce my prednisone one-half milligram at a time. I stay on the new dosage a few weeks, and then go down another half milligram until I bottom out. I use the miracle lamp regularly. Like most longtime arthritics, I start getting dry eyes and add a bottle of artificial tears to the cornucopia of my medicine cabinet.

Wei and I are preparing for retirement. It's hard for him to think of quitting. My feeling is good-bye to the drudgery of yesteryears, and the hot, humid subway rides in the summer!

There's still a mountain of tidying and packing and discarding and moving left to do. So hello, aching backs and sore limbs, too.

In August I have another surgery on my left foot, but it's ambulatory, so at least I don't have to sit around in a wheelchair for hours staring at the scratched-up linoleum. Count your blessings. There's just a little pain, which I take in stride (even though the stride hurts).

Mexico! The Mexican Riviera cruise—the glass-bottom boat shows the beauties of underwater mountains. "Mexican chickens"—otherwise knows as pelicans—perch all over on the rocks of the gulf like little guardian statues.

Wei has hernia surgery. It goes perfectly, and he's grateful for how fast my dietary supplements help him heal.

We have a wonderful family Christmas. Anthony is almost overwhelmed with excitement, and my Chateaubriand is devoured with gusto. Peace on Earth to all.

1992. Now on to my deformed and crooked hands. I meet with Dr. H., one of the world's best hand surgeons. I like him right away, and after talking to him I trust him as well. We schedule the surgeries so I can finish tax returns and go to China in the fall.

A month later, I enter the hospital and get a private room. (I'm learning!) The surgery (right hand) goes well, and the cast comes off a month later.

It is time for hand therapy, which is tedious and painful, but oh so good for me. In a month, Dr. H. takes all three pins out and praises me for my therapy progress.

I still need a splint to protect the hand and a night splint to help my ring finger. I've been typing for my diary since the surgery, but now I try writing again. It's hard to hold the pen, but patience and practice (and shorter sentences) helps me to once again write down my days as I've done all my life.

A month later, I get surgery to fix my three fingertips that don't bend. And here's something: the ten Novocain (and two antibiotic) injections directly into my hand give me more pain than anything I've ever encountered in my "pain's my middle name" life! Lord!

It's called an area block procedure, and *my* procedure is to *block* it out of the area of my memory as soon as I can! In four days, I don't need strong pain pills any more. The third, fourth, and fifth fingers are bandaged, and my hand's in a sling, but I still can cook and type with my remaining digits and left hand. Somehow I manage. In a month I'm writing in my diary again. What do I write? What you've just read! A sentence that sums up the story of my life: *"Somehow I manage."*

Now I start planning my high school reunion in earnest. It's next year (our fiftieth since graduating in 1943), and there are many letters to write. I have an idea—a weeklong cruise, a grand plan maybe, but it was a grand class.

In the fall, I go to China for seven weeks with Wei and Elaine, my two favorite travel companions. It's a fantastic time, and my new feet and hand are up to the trip. It doesn't exhaust me because we have our own guide and a very flexible schedule. (A tour group would be much too demanding and strenuous.) My high school is having a general reunion (its centennial celebration), so I get to see many of my schoolmates from all over the world. We visit all the renowned wonders and historical sites of China. Revisiting Shanghai and the places of my childhood there and showing them to Wei and Elaine moves me the most. When I see those mountains again and breathe deep of that precious air, I feel my heart fill with gratitude for the beauty that God gives to all.

Our trip is seven glorious weeks and covers Beijing, Xian, Shanghai, Shuzhou, Wuxi, Hangzhow, Nanking, Kunming, Canton, and Hong Kong! Walking is the main method of transportation—lots of walking. The most strenuous trek goes miles and miles through the famous Rock Forest in Kunming. During this Olympian event, I get the feeling over and over again that maybe on this finite world I've actually found somewhere endless! But no—it finally, finally, *finally* ends after a number of hours. Nevertheless, it is so breathtakingly beautiful.

Home again, and there are stacks of mail from the classmates I contacted—everyone's so excited! My hands get quite a workout answering them all.

I visit my sister. She's fading fast, but her mind is still clear, and I know she's glad to see me.

Her suffering ends on Christmas day. I have many memories of her to cherish, but I feel inconsolable. The Lord gives, and the Lord takes away. God only knows why. So be it. Sometimes all we can do is bow our heads.

1993. Right before surgery for my left hand, I shower (which always helps my arthritis) and do a miracle lamp treatment. However, with my dear Aunt M.'s illness and my sister's interment occupying my mind, I've forgotten to take extra vitamin B6 for two weeks before surgery. Because of this, my recovery from the surgery is rockier than before and includes nausea and vomiting. That'll teach me to forget my B6.

However, because of the excellence of my general health, I still recover quickly. Somehow I manage! Music—as always—smoothes my recuperation, and I start reducing my prednisone.

The cast is sawed off a month after surgery, but the pins have to stay in for a while. I have a hand splint and bi-weekly therapy sessions. The hand looks ugly all stitched up and scarred, but at least it looks like a hand now. When the stitches come out, the scar is painful, but rubbing vitamin E on it helps a great deal. One fine summer day, I have my first manicure in almost thirty years! What a treat.

Up and down, life goes on. Wei goes on Coumadin for an irregular heartbeat. Elaine's friend, Bob, calls us and asks for our blessing in marrying our daughter. This is good news indeed!

Our high school reunion cruise—the Caribbean! During the cruise, my class honors me with a session of singing, Chinese poetry, and a photo collection to thank me for organizing it all. We're all one big, happy, laughing family. When we talk about our high school times, we're suddenly teens again, squealing and shouting and laughing like teenagers. So much laughter! It's great to see everyone so happy. We resolve to do it again every two years.

1994. I have a thirteen-minute surgery on my left hand. It is not too painful, and I experience a speedy healing. The hand is starting to look good. A month later, another minor surgery on my left foot—this time there's pain, but pain pills take care of it.

Up, down, and sideways—we're preparing for Elaine and Bob's wedding, and book Tavern on the Green for the reception. My dear Aunt M. suffers through her last months: a broken hip, a dead intestine, and finally a ruptured aneurysm. She dies February 17. There goes another precious person. Even though she was a distant aunt, she always showed unwavering confidence in me. I always felt heartened by her. It's extra sad because she was so looking forward to attending Elaine's wedding.

October 8: A perfect day—the ceremony's at Christ Church on Park Avenue, and ten-year-old Tarryn is beautiful and poised as the junior bridesmaid. An antique horse-drawn carriage takes the bride and groom to the reception. Elaine changes into a purple Chantilly Chinese gown for dancing. She's gorgeous.

Delicious food! Jubilant dancing! Many guests tell me it's the best wedding they've ever attended. Why should I argue? I'm just happy I could help make everything just right for my beautiful, dear Elaine.

Eugene, Mia, Tarryn, Alyson, Anthony, Elaine, and Bob join us for a December cruise on the Eastern Caribbean to celebrate Wei's eightieth birthday and my seventieth. The children have a ball, and the adults always seem to be smiling.

1995, January–August. Under my doctor's advice, I no longer have massages. One session gives my arm a large lump, caused by broken vessels; and another puts incapacitating pain in my thigh. Massage can be wonderful, but the masseuse cannot use regular strength on a body made fragile by RA.

My disease has also left me with little cartilage in my right knee, which pains me to no end. I meet with a knee specialist for yet another surgery. Doctor S., a renowned orthopedic surgeon, is friendly and warm, instantly putting me at ease. I have a notebook full of questions, but his explanations are so good I don't need to ask a thing. Somehow, after Dr. S. explains my upcoming surgery, I'm completely confident and optimistic about the procedure. I've never met a doctor like him!

It's major surgery, but it goes smoothly. The next day, they remove the heavy cast, but leave in the IV, epidural needle, and catheter. A physical therapist comes to dangle my legs. I use the CPM (continual passive motion) machine for three hours.

On day two, I amaze everyone by bending my knee seventy-five degrees and walking around with a cane.

On day three, my tubes are removed, except for an IV in my right hand. A blood clot is found in my calf, which is typical with knee surgery because of the tourniquets used in the operation. I'm put on Coumadin. I bend my knee ninety-five degrees and hobble up four steps. The doctors can't believe how well I'm doing.

On day four, it's a hundred and five degrees. The therapist says she's never seen such improvement in anyone before.

On day five, I go home with thirty-four staples in my leg. Three days later, they're pulled out one by one, but my leg now feels much lighter and more flexible.

I rest a lot and take iron because of all the blood I lost in surgery. The therapist, lab technician, and nurse visit daily to check my progress. In a week I can take a shower by myself. A few more weeks, and I'm off Coumadin and don't need the technician to draw blood any more. That's a relief!

The therapist says she'll be coming three times a week for six more weeks. After three weeks, she smiles and says her work is over. Doctor S. says my recovery was spectacular, and I'm his number one patient.

A month and a half later, I walk fifteen blocks and my knee doesn't make a peep! No more pain, and extra mobility.

Seventy-one years old, and I'm a new woman!

CHAPTER 9

HARVEST

1995–1998. Sometimes in life, you get the chance to reap the rewards of your work and sacrifice. These years are harvest years for Wei Foo and me, with the time, health, and resources to travel and see our friends and family and the world. Even though we know hard times will come, how can we not be thankful for such a period of grace?

In September, we start preparing for something I've been wanting for a long time: a new kitchen—a complete remodeling! Emptying all the cabinets is, to put it nicely, "breathtaking." Climbing the ladder, up and down, repeatedly, then packing and moving the boxes—it is strenuous, but I make sure to give myself ample time and space at every stage to minimize all physical and mental stress and strain.

I find Wei's mind quite confused during this time. Normally, he pitches in without being asked. But I find this usually helpful person no longer available. Somehow, I'll manage—and I do.

1995, October. The demolition starts, and the workers are here every day. By mid-November we have a whole new kitchen, back room floor, and back bathroom. Beautiful! Then there is more unpacking and stacking. There is a lot of pain, but all is well again.

November. Wei and I go on a Mississippi River cruise. We take a plane to New Orleans first and tour the city for three days. Dinner on the balcony with street musicians playing on the street below is very enjoyable and relaxing. Life in New Orleans bustles like in New York City, but in an entirely different way. The whole experience is enlightening.

Then on to the *American Queen* steamboat, chugging down the mighty Mississippi at eight miles per hour, I go for the hot Cajun food and touch a three-year-old gator.

I'm surprised by a steamboat birthday party Wei has arranged for me. I am so touched by his thoughtfulness. I didn't know he had that kind of organizational energy anymore, but he does! This elegant, soft-smiling guy truly loves me.

We keep traveling. In December, we go to California for Wei's niece's wedding. Elaine and Bob join us. We take the opportunity to visit the Paul Getty Museum in Malibu and Disneyland. I notice that Wei shows no interest in any activity. After the wedding, we go to Las Vegas. We go to one show where six drums are playing, loud and exciting. I look at Wei. He's fast asleep.

Every time Wei and I go on a cruise, Wei can be found where the food is. Even after three big meals and afternoon tea, he still seems to be hungry again at the midnight buffet. If anybody wants to find me after dinner and the evening show, I can be found playing blackjack, my favorite game, in the ship's casino. I lose some, then switch tables and win $150. The dealers tell me, "You're good!" I never take a credit card—too tempting. If I lose $100, I quit; if I win around $150, I quit. My discipline in fighting RA serves me well in winning blackjack! Over the years I've been playing, I'm way ahead.

When we return, it's 1996. Happy New Year, happy old years!

In February, it's on to Milwaukee for my friend's son's wedding. They are long and happy days. Then we drop by Michigan to visit Eugene, Mia, and the kids. They've grown! Obvious, I know, but still—it always seems surprising.

Back home, I start taking Catherine's Choice Aloe Vera Capsules. I start slowly and gradually increase the dose. As I am hoping, it helps me reduce my prednisone. I'm happy and very encouraged.

I test my strength with my old ritual of cleaning the blinds in the tub. "Take it slow, one at a time. Don't stress your hands or elbows," I tell myself. My joints pronounce success. I'm happier and encouraged.

I'm reducing my prednisone to the lowest levels ever: from nine, to eight, and then seven milligrams, and two ibuprofens! I add doses of glucosamine, an amino sugar that reduces the inflammation of joints, but quit after an itch develops. Later I try taking chondroitin with the glucosamine, and this combination works very well. Never stop looking for ways to feel better!

We travel to the American West—Utah and Mormon history—the incomprehensible hate they endured. Wyoming has arches of antelope horns and food as good as the view. Old Faithful in Yellowstone erupts twice for Wei and me. It is nice of it to do so. We have quail for dinner. We have lunch at Irma's, named after Wild Bill's daughter. South Dakota—only 675,000 people! Mount Rushmore—magnificent!

Another old ritual: painting the living room. With all the work before and after moving the glassware and precious antiques in and out of the cabinets, and even with reduced prednisone, I'm doing well. Prayers of thanksgiving flow easily.

Our second reunion cruise with classmates, friends, and relatives gets off to a rocky start with the ship not showing up on time! But things work out—the captain even speaks to me in Chinese—and we all like the Panama Canal. We plan our next cruise for Egypt, but when they start shooting tourists there, we change it to the Blue Danube.

The Blue Danube Waltz is lovely to hear played live in its birthplace, Vienna. On board the cruise ship MVII *Blue Danube*, the same lovely music surrounds us, and the captain and staff are terrific. We tour Buda *and* Pest! We go to Kalosca, paprika capital of the world—everyone buys paprika. We see a wild Mongolian horse-riding show. Abbey Melk gilded in gold from top to bottom.

Back in the States, Wei and I take Tarryn and Alyson to see my old friend, the Statue of Liberty. Wei rests in the park while we three ladies start climbing the 354 steps to the crown. The last 140 steps were very, very narrow in the spiral stairway.

We all make it without any problems.

As I gaze out at the beautiful harbor and the shore of hope for so many over the years—smiling at my granddaughter's happy exclamations—I feel incomparably proud. When I first got RA, I remember fearing that such a view would never be mine again. Yet here I am, living proof that there's freedom from the oppression of RA.

I'm thankful for these last years—always glowing in my memory, like my eyes on the day I looked out from the crown of Lady Liberty.

I've reached a point with my arthritis when I feel very well some days. The next day, I know, my RA can still strike deep. Good weather, healthy food intake, rest, a relaxing shower, a positive mental state, and limiting my physical work—all contribute to my well-being.

Wei now seems to be growing more and more confused each month. When he loses his keys, he gets violently upset. I buy him an extra long keychain. When I fix it firmly on the buckle of his pants, he calms down. Compassion and attention are what's best for him now—and creatively tending his worries.

He sees a neurologist who runs him through a variety of tests. All the results are negative—except for the verbal test. The diagnosis: Alzheimer's.

CHAPTER 10

WRESTLING THE WHIRLWIND

About twenty years ago, Wei and I saw a movie about a memory-swallowing dementia called Alzheimer's. Both of us were struck by how devastating this disease was. There's no cure, and the downhill process can last for many torturous years.

Starting in 1993, I found Wei unusually confused at times. I requested an MRI, but it showed nothing that might indicate a problem. The confusion since then has crept up slowly but steadily, and now it is undeniable.

Wei is eighty-three when he's diagnosed and starts taking Aricept. This helps his memory a little, but only for the first stage of Alzheimer's. Even this early—when the victim can get extremely angry and obstinate with the changes and fears that come with loss of memory and orientation—things can get very rough. But compared to the later stages, the first stage is not so bad.

I know I'm in for a long ordeal, but I will do whatever God gives me the strength and compassion to do. The beast of RA has given me tough training in fighting a devastating disease.

I know the stress and physical labor I'll no doubt encounter will now push my RA to the limits. I'm glad I've kept my health up over the years so I can fight this battle, and I will. I love this man. He's been unstintingly patient and helpful to me all these years with my RA. I'll do everything for him.

It turns out, everything is exactly what I will have to do.

1998, November. We spend three weeks in Michigan taking care of the grandkids while Eugene and Mia go to China, realizing a lifelong dream they share. Wei is acting as childish as the children and wants to go home. Somehow I manage.

> **Early Signs of Alzheimer's Disease**
>
> - Short-term memory loss (forgetting recent events and conversations, forgetting new information)
> - Misplacing belongings in unusual places
> - Questionable judgment (wearing summer clothes on a cold day, extravagant spending)
> - Decline in abstract thinking (problems with mental arithmetic, trouble with planning daily life)
> - Problems with everyday tasks (forgetting how to do a favorite pastime, forgetting how to do simple daily routines)
> - Personality changes (fearful, suspicious, or confused behavior)
> - Unusual mood changes
> - Difficulty with language (using unusual words or forgetting simple ones)
> - Disorientation (forgetting what day it is, getting lost in very familiar places)
> - Passivity (sleeping more than usual, disinterest in favorite activities)

Back home, our regular routine calms Wei down, but he still refuses to listen to my suggestions. He gets especially confused at night (a symptom called *sundowning*), and demands all the compassion I can muster. It's wearying and sad. My RA swells, and my patience wears thin.

Eating at restaurants seems to be the one thing we can rely on Wei liking. I'm not too keen about this hobby of his, but I oblige. The precious hour or so of happiness it gives him is worth it, and I can relax a bit too, which is very important.

December 26. Our fiftieth wedding anniversary is sadly not so golden, but it is what it is, and for that I am thankful.

Only our immediate family is here to celebrate, because large crowds make Wei confused and upset. Before the dinner, I stand to say a prayer I've prepared, but then I'm too overcome with emotion. Wei's condition saddens me profoundly. I manage to say only a few words and leave it to God and my loved ones to fill in the rest. This certainly is not what I expected, and that is fast becoming the theme of this chapter of my life.

December 30. Around two in the morning, Wei comes to my room saying some intruder woke him up. I go with him to his room and lie down with him a while. At first, he babbles about the intruder, but then starts asking with intense concern: *How can I be changing so much?* My heart goes out to him. The next morning he remembers me lying down with him when he was confused. He holds my hand and tells me how happy he is with me.

1999, January. We celebrate Wei's eighty-fourth birthday at a Chinese restaurant, which makes him very happy. His mood changes are hard to predict. I listen to music a lot to keep my sanity. I try to reduce my prednisone, but it doesn't work—too much stress. I have to stay as stable as I can, so I keep it at its former level.

February. Chinese New Year's Eve, I do the hot pot tradition, but Wei forgets his tradition of putting an orange in every room. He always used to help, but now he's not in any way helpful. Mostly he's in a daze. Sadness and tension have become our new houseguests.

June. In the morning, Wei asks me if I'm his wife. I say, "Yes. You're Mr. Chun, and I'm Mrs. Chun. Eugene and Elaine are our children." He chews on this. I always try to exercise his mind whenever I can.

September. Wei thinks intruders are stealing things. He hides many things and forgets where he hid them. He has to sleep with a light on, and always puts his wallet under his pillow.

October. Wei can no longer find his way around our neighborhood or change the clocks for daylight savings time.

November. Wei likes to turn on every light in the apartment. This is annoying. Then for a few weeks, I hear him humming and singing as he cleans up. This is lovely.

November 30, 4:30 AM. Wei opens my door looking very distressed. "Come lie down with me," I say. He does and tells me he's been looking all over the apartment for me. He is afraid I had left him. He was smart enough, however, to look in the closet and see that all my coats were there. He kept looking and found food in the fridge. He wondered how he could cook for himself. Then he just sat at the dining table looking at a cup of tea and cried. "Where could I go? Who could I call?" He is so frightened. I'm choked up. "I'll never leave you," I tell him. "You can feel safe." I tell him how to speed-dial our son or daughter or our neighbors if he needs to call someone. But I know he won't remember. It's a nightmare of helpless love.

December. I help him shower now and wash his hair. He smiles and jokes. I feel so happy.

He tells me he just saw my face and figures he's seen me before.

For a while, he shaves six times a day, like a pastime. Now I have to urge him to shave.

I'm not getting enough sleep. My head is pounding, and he comes in my room very early in the morning and says, "Let's get something to eat and get moving." He does this two days in a row, saying the same exact words.

Now giving him a shower and washing his hair is a big problem. His resistance is so forceful that it physically wears me down. If I don't handle it tactfully, his anger explodes.

Somehow I manage.

"Today's our wedding anniversary," I tell him. He looks at me blankly.

On New Year's Eve, I watch the crystal ball come down alone. If ever I need faith, the time is now. God will not give me a cross too heavy to carry.

2000. Wei has gained sixteen pounds. I don't think he knows whether he's hungry or full.

He's become a creature of the night. I hear his shaver buzzing at 2:00 AM. At half-past four, he wakes me and insists we go and eat. I tell him the only things open are a supermarket and a copy place, and that he could be robbed or hurt by people lurking in the night. There's also lots of food and snacks already in our home. I can see he's going out no matter what I say, but he's worried he'll get hurt. I go along with him and buy a little something at the supermarket. This seems to be all he needs. By the time we're home again, it's 6:00 AM. It is another night of far too little sleep for me.

Wei now sleeps an hour or two at a time—day or night, and I must watch him and do daily business for our home and welfare. Rest has always been my main defense against RA attacks. I'm courting bodily disaster by taking care of Wei, but what else can I do? It's too soon to hire a nurse.

Wei floods the back bathroom and part of the back room.

I tell Wei that his birthday's coming, and he asks me for a party. This makes me very happy. The small group I gather at his favorite Chinese restaurant makes *him* very happy.

I notice Wei is walking funny. I find his left side black and blue, and it's painful to the touch. He must've hurt it falling off the scale two days ago. He never said a thing. Thank God, X-rays show no fracture.

At night, he likes to put his walking shoes on and stomp around, angry and belligerent. In the mornings now, he's not so sure of where he is, but tells me often, "I'm so lucky that I have you."

Many times at dawn, I go lie down with him, and we talk.

I hear him singing to himself for quite a while today.

Two Asian men, he says, slept in his bed last night.

The two bed-jumpers are back, he informs me.

"Are they Chinese?" I ask. "Filipinos? Malaysians?"

"How would I know?" he responds. "All I know is that they're homeless."

Wei must think he has a new night job. His assignment: stomping around like a soldier and flushing toilets.

I'm so frazzled these days, my Chinese New Year hot pot seems to be an awful lot of work. But Wei devours it so happily, it lifts my spirits.

I find him going downstairs with his hat, shoes, and gloves on, but wearing pajamas with his long keychain around his neck.

I play music for him every day. This afternoon he clapped and danced along for quite some time. I can still hear him laughing and humming, although the CD ended half an hour ago.

His strong resentment at taking his medicine and vitamins weakens his resistance to showering. You win some, you lose some.

"What's your name?"

"Wei Foo Chun."

"What's mine?"

"Anita Chun."

I tell myself these lucid moments will not last, but still they make me feel like crying with happiness.

He floods the bathroom again. Elaine is here, and she cleans up. I keep a big stack of newspapers in the bathroom now.

Wei greets me this morning with, "Hi, Mom." He hasn't called me that in months.

He went out today without letting me know. I tell him I always let him know when I go out, even just to get the mail, and he should do the same. I can see him make the effort to stick this in his memory. Only problem is—how much stickiness is left in there?

I find him trying to put his legs in the sleeves of his jacket.

April 1. He tells me he's found something strange on his body, hairs that never were there before. He does not suddenly smile and say, "April Fool!"

At the restaurant, he doesn't know what the foods are. For some reason, this is particularly sad to me. After dinner, we walk to the market next door, and I show him the foods. He's interested.

Wei has growing paranoia now, which is a common symptom of Alzheimer's second stage. Anything he can't find, he thinks someone took. He starts hiding things more and more and finding them less and less. What a vicious circle!

Wei tells me his wife has left him. "Call our friends to find her! Without her, I get very sad!" I ask him who I am. He gets a very troubled look and says, "My wife."

He gives the back bathroom yet another soak.

Although he hasn't gone out, he says he's just had lunch at a Chinese restaurant. "What did you have? Did you leave a tip?" I ask. "That's my business," he says. He probably wishes he could go out solo. What man doesn't?

"I feel lonesome," he tells me.

We take a half-hour bus ride to a community center that welcomes Alzheimer's victims and offers watercoloring, bingo, playing ball, exercise, and a hot lunch. Wei needs persuasion to join. I keep him company, hoping to ease my way out in the future.

I need surgery to correct a bone in my big toe. I know I'll have to elevate my foot after the surgery, so before I have surgery I try to finish all the work I need to do around the house. The night before the surgery, Wei puts down the stopper in the bathroom sink and turns the taps on full force. As I clean up the flood, Wei angrily rants that he had nothing to do with the mess. It's weird, but I'm actually grateful to him for doing it tonight rather than after my surgery.

Our cleaning lady takes care of Wei while I have my minor surgery. I'm able to hold off on my pain pill till 7:30 PM.

I try to elevate my foot as much as possible, but Wei is becoming incontinent. I clean it up as matter-of-factly as I can in order not to shame him.

The insurance adjuster comes to inspect the water damage caused by Wei's last flood. It's not too bad. The inspector's sympathetic because his mother-in-law also has Alzheimer's.

My foot takes over a month to heal, and every night Wei slams his door in great distress. I wonder just how long I can take care of him.

Thoughts come into my mind to help me cope with Wei's condition. *I should not compare him with his old self because they're two different people. I should consider myself as a volunteer taking care of a person in need.* These two points console me. I'm also honoring my marriage vow—in sickness and in health—just as he did, as long as he was able. My love for Wei is unconditional and forever.

At 3:00 AM, then 4:00 AM, Wei comes in my room and announces, "We are having a new day now." I have to laugh. I tell him I start my new day a few hours later than he does.

Live music and lots of dancing today at the community center. I get Wei to dance with me. He wears a long face the entire time, but I know he secretly enjoys it.

I try leaving him alone at the center. Before an hour passes, I get a call informing me he's looking for me all over the place. I go back. This is the first time since his diagnosis he's ever been without me.

I bring Wei to the center at 10:30 AM. I draw a clock on a yellow card with the short hand on 2 and the long hand on 6 and tell him that's when I'll be back. There are no calls this time. I pick him up at 2:30 PM and treat him to apple pie *a la mode,* his favorite snack.

Wei can't quite recall his grandchildren's names, but, in his own way, I know he misses them as much as I do. We fly to Michigan. Eugene and Alyson greet us. Wei thinks Eugene is his friend, not his son, and this won't change. At one point in our weeklong visit, Elaine and Bob join us. He can't recall their names either, but the warm family feelings can't be erased and make it a good visit for us.

When I ask him who I am, he calls me Madame Chun in Chinese. Sometimes he can't even think of his own name, but one thing he never forgets is that he was an architect. He hugs his album with all the projects he worked on in his productive life.

Everyone at the center goes to the beach. He enjoys the change.

More nighttime fun—he's slamming the wall, moving things out of his closet, and turning his phone upside down. He says someone else did it.

He's furious when I pick him up at the center. He's been looking all over for me and "will never go through that again!"

More wee-hour floods in the bathroom occur. He also visits the doorman in underwear and socks.

There is a huge incontinence accident at the center. I take him home, clean him up, and call the doctor to decrease his medication.

Terrible mood changes and strange behavior occur. He throws unwanted foods on the floor in the restaurant. He bangs on the piano any time of day or night. He slams the wall, slams doors, screams like a coyote, and barks like a dog. Then he'll suddenly smile and tell me he likes me. I turn on music to calm down his poor suffering soul. I pray for strength and patience every day.

Three in the morning seems to be his magic time to see if he can empty the entire New York City water supply into our bathroom. After the deluge, he curiously watches me fill eight garbage bags with wet newspapers.

This time he floods it when I go out for a bit. Somehow he manages to get the super to clean it up! That is smart of him.

I find him talking to himself and to the photos of the family on the piano.

In the restaurant, he hands me part of what he's eating and asks me to return it and get the cost deducted from our bill.

New medication. He's calmer, but talks and talks—mostly complaints and unpleasant hallucinations.

He doesn't know if it's night or day. Even looking out the window at the daylight can't convince him that it's morning.

Increasing incontinence plagues him. He tries a new medication. A few days later, he blurts out, "It's making me quiet!" This is evidence of something I suspected all along: *He knows more than we give him credit for.*

He has difficulty walking. A CAT scan shows no bleeding or stroke. I take him to buy a cane. He storms out of the store. I carry the cane home.

I get him to use the cane, and he walks much better. I compliment him on it—positive reinforcement.

My optimism turns out to be wishful thinking. Soon he's twirling his cane around like a toy and hitting things. I have to hide it to prevent accidents.

Dear Lord, Wei is such a sweet man, and he's deteriorating right in front me. He's living in anxiety, insecurity, and sheer misery. My tough old heart is breaking like glass. I know everything happens for a reason, but I still do not get the message!

Major changes occur. Wei no longer grabs the newspaper first thing in the morning to underline passages in red. In addition, he is wearing Depends, which don't always prevent the need for mammoth clean-ups. I won't go into detail, but these get increasingly frequent and awful.

Here's a new way of flooding the bathroom: plug the toilet with a whole roll of toilet paper and flush like there's no tomorrow. One improvement: now he kind of apologetically admits he did it.

Did you know there are other people living with us? I didn't. But Wei won't let me forget it.

Here's another thing Wei tells me about that I didn't know: His wife has been gone for two weeks!

At 2:00 AM, I'm awakened by a booming voice talking with Wei. You mean there *is* someone living with us? Nevertheless, Wei is alone when I find him, his wallet sticking out of his pajama pocket: "The doorman helped me." Our night doorman has a big voice. I call him up, and he tells me he found Wei in the lobby not knowing how to get home. He brought him back and found our doormat holding the door open.

I get new locks on our doors that I can lock from the inside.

I have a small birthday party for myself in a nice restaurant. It's important not to give up everything.

Wei tells me he can't find himself. I tell him to touch his body. He does. His face lights up.

"Where's the bedroom?"

"Where the photos of your grandchildren are."

"Ah. Where's my room?"

"Where your big drafting table is."

"I know. But how do I fall asleep?"

"Just lie down and close your eyes."

He does.

He never goes anywhere without his wallet. He guards it as if it's his very life force. The $45 he keeps in it makes him feel very rich. So whenever he asks me why the doors are locked—which he asks every time he tries them—the answer that satisfies him best is "So no one can get in to steal your money."

When he sleeps or naps now, he turns on the ceiling light and wears sunglasses. He's a cool cat.

December. All along, he's been asking, "When can we go on another cruise?" Our reunion group wants to see Egypt now that it's safe for tourists. Our doctors advise against it, but I know it's Wei's last chance. Because of all the extra work Wei gives me, the doctors are more concerned about my health than Wei's, but I know: *Somehow I'll manage.* We go.

It's a blessing, this trip. Everyone enjoys it. The kindness of people helps us make it. Our friends and tour guides do special favors for us, like giving us the front seats on the bus, closest to the doors. Whenever a major attraction requires a lot of walking, a young man helps Wei into a wheelchair and pushes him around so we both can join the group.

One of the moments I'll never forget occurs as Wei and I are relaxing in the bus while the others shop. A smiling, stout man with a turban climbs on the bus and comes right to me. He stands there smiling with the darkest, brightest eyes I've ever seen. He looks so brilliantly at me. He never looks once at Wei. Suddenly he pulls out an Egyptian five-pound note and puts it on the tray in front of me. Keeping his smile, still looking at me, he pulls out one more and puts that on the tray by the other one. Then, before I can catch my breath, he's gone from the bus and walking down the street as I watch in wonder. He suddenly turns and waves right at me, then vanishes completely from sight.

Then I realize it's Ramadan, when people make it a point to be especially kind and charitable. The Egyptian money was maybe worth only a few U.S. dollars, but I know it could buy a great deal of pita, their daily bread.

I sit there with a smile on my face that reaches back to the smiles on the faces of those ten-year-olds we gave donuts to, the smile on my father's face when I told him of the money I gave to my school friend, the smile on the face of the American lady showing me the near-empty rice barrel, and who knows—it feels like it could be the same smile my mother gave me when I was first put into her arms.

Back home, I get the two bills framed and hang them in my bedroom. How hard this new millennium has been for me so far! In 2000 I lost eight dear friends. And I can't even begin to count how many times I had to clean up the flood. But as I look at the framed bills, I also feel grateful for being able to care for my husband. Even though I rarely get the sleep I need, I haven't had to increase my RA medication. Lord, you know what you're doing even if I don't.

Thank you for all you've given me—that I know about and that I don't know about—and for all you'll have to give me to get through the dark days I know lie ahead.

CHAPTER 11

WANTING IT OVER, DREADING HIM GONE

So far it's been easy, compared to what's coming. This could be the motto for Alzheimer's caregivers.

Let me tell you, we're a special breed. It's small compensation for the hell we go through, but one thing we can say proudly: *we earn our stripes.*

The awareness that bad things will keep getting worse gives me the same mortal fear I felt when I first learned I had RA, and, just as I did when I was twenty-five, I vow to stay the course because my love "out-Wei's" the disease.

2001. This year Wei does not request a birthday celebration. This year he does not even know what a birthday is.

It's getting too much for me, especially his many ways of robbing me of sleep. Friends, family, and doctors suggest a nursing home, but I don't have the heart for that. He loves Chinese food, which the homes don't provide. Even though he doesn't remember our relationship, without me there for him, he goes crazy. I can't throw him into the void. That would make this terrible time even worse for him.

It would also shorten his life. It's so strange. Wretched as all this has been for me, I don't want my Wei to leave me.

I pray for guidance. The doctor prescribes melatonin to help his sleep. I begin looking for a Chinese man to help me five or six days a week.

During this time I'm inspired to write this book. I don't see how I can with all my caretaking work and the little I know about writing—but this little seed of fire takes root in me. It plants a quiet, new energy in my life. *Somehow I'll manage.*

I call Mrs. L., who knows many Chinese people. She sends me Mr. C., a Chinese man with a wife and five children and experience tending an invalid. He likes working here in the States and is willing to start right away, but I know he wants to see his sons in Hong Kong for the Chinese New Year. "Start when you come back," I suggest, and he agrees.

I come back from the hairdresser's, and Wei tells our cleaning lady, "The best is back." How can I give up a guy like this?

"What's your name?" he asks me today.

"Anita Chun."

"My name is also Chun! Wei Foo Chun."

At least he knows his name.

I try to stop him from playing with the Norman Rockwell plates hanging on the wall. He gets violent, as he often does now when he doesn't get his way. This time my thumb is injured. It swells up and turns blue. I can't take it much longer—the bowel accidents, his refusal to take medicine. My elbows and arms are killing me from pushing and pulling him. When is Mr. C. coming back?

Mrs. L. tells me Mr. C.'s two Hong Kong sons don't think he should work any more, so they took his plane ticket away. She sends me Mr. L., a pleasant man in his forties who doesn't speak a word of English. We set his schedule for five days a week, seven hours a day.

His first day he's too attentive to Wei, and Wei gives him such a look.

I suggest he warm up to Wei more gradually. I show him how to shower Wei and wash his hair.

Wei starts getting used to him, and I start getting some relief. Nevertheless, Wei always comes looking for me, and I need some time to myself. So I send them every day for lunch at a Chinese restaurant, which Wei always enjoys. On the days I join them, he's exceedingly happy. He wants me around all the time.

At 2:00 AM a *"boom, boom, boom, boom"* wakes me up. It's Wei trying to open the locked kitchen door. He won't give up. He has a can of nuts and a tin of butter cookies in a pillowcase ready to go. It's pretty smart of him to have food ready to take along. His face is all red, and he's very agitated. "I have to go see this place being built! If I'm late, I'll miss the opportunity!" I can't calm him down. "Lord," I ask, "help me."

I mix him a cider and Benadryl cocktail. He refuses to drink it. I turn on the TV to distract him and sit down to sew a bed skirt. He finally sits and starts to nod off. By 3:30 AM I get him to drink the cider—another quiet evening at home.

I find him telling the sofa how much he enjoys sitting on it.

He's more and more incontinent. I tell him it's natural to use the toilet but not natural to do it on the floor. Later, sitting on the toilet, he says, "This is natural." He remembers!

But it doesn't last, and the accidents get worse. Cleaning up a huge late-night episode causes me unbearable wrist pain the next morning, an arthritis attack just like the old days. Wei is also showing signs of not walking so well but refuses to let me help him, which causes increasing stress on my joints. I have to take extra ibuprofen.

We finally get him a wheelchair. He likes it! I start to feel almost like myself again.

From 10:00 PM on, Wei violently refuses his medication. The second time he pushes me down, I get a big lump on my head, even though the floor is carpeted. I just lie there to see what he'll do. I'm very curious! I have to do something for entertainment, or I'll go crazy. He stoops down shyly to touch me, probably to see if I'm still alive. Now he looks cute. I smile at him and he looks even cuter.

I find a comb in his diaper. Twice before, I found a roll of toilet paper.

He wasn't kidding when he told the sofa he likes to sit on it. The problem now is he can't get up from it. I have to push and pull, just as he and little Eugene used to do to me to get me out of bed almost fifty years ago. My left elbow is developing a constant pain from this activity.

Wei can't even walk one block any more. I expect to see deterioration, but it always seems to be too much too soon. The signs of his failing health bring tears to my eyes almost daily now. I still keep praying for Christ to restore his brain cells. *Lord, aren't all things possible with you? But your will be done.*

His legs are much weaker, but still he struggles to walk. He can't, but he doesn't give up. I just try to keep him from taking a fall.

I will always love his fighting spirit and his drive to be independent.

He loves ice cream with nuts. Now he holds the nuts in his mouth and just eats the ice cream. He's having trouble chewing things. It takes me a while to get the nuts from his mouth, but I don't want him to choke. From now on, it's only plain chocolate ice cream, which he has every night. Since he spits out pills, I melt the pills and put the solution in the chocolate ice cream to make sure he takes his medicine.

Sometimes I find him on the floor when no help is there. I have to get a doorman or porter to help. People can be so kind.

I have to get him up off the sofa to go to the bathroom and to bed, but he's fighting me tooth and nail. My arms and elbows pulse with fire. I put my arms around him from behind and try again. He pushes me down on the hardwood floor, and I drag him down with me. My right hip and knee are locked in pain, and he's lying on his back crying out softly, "Help, help..." I have to find a way to get up for him.

I look around for something to pull myself up with. Nothing. I pray my most basic prayer: "God, help." I pull down a big cushion and crawl onto it for elevation, then wiggle my way up onto the couch. Then I sit, stand, and call down for a doorman who comes up and rescues Wei. *Pretty good trick,* I tell myself, feeling strangely happy—thank you, Lord, and thank you, doorman.

I have to get someone to help in the night. The holding and lifting and tugging and pushing are wreaking pure hell on my RA. The added stress from such exertion causes seemingly incessant RA flare-ups. Today I am behind him to keep him from falling, but he starts to fall forward, and my arms are too weak to prevent it. If he falls on his head, it will just be too awful, so without thinking I pinch him on the back. This straightens him backward, which gives me a chance to wrap my arms around him and waltz him safely into his room. Thank God! While I rest on his bed and he sits in a chair, he asks me, "How do you feel?" This normal question surprises me like the Sun bursting through clouds.

The doctor tells me Wei is approaching the third stage of Alzheimer's, so he takes him off the Aricept. No medicine can help his condition now.

He likes to watch more TV now. While watching Reverend Schuller on the *Hour of Power,* Wei says, "He's a good man. Let's give him all our money."

With some shows, he feels like he's actually *in* what he's watching and screams like a child at the scary scenes.

He can hardly stand now. My eyes ache from the sadness, and my thigh and hip ache from holding him up. I've hardly slept for ages. I'm exhausted, and it's hard not to be cranky. It's time for twenty-four-hour care, so Mr. L. starts living with us.

I get a hospital bed for Wei and hire someone for Mr. L.'s day off. The newcomer acts like a guest, but we'll just have to get used to it.

September 11. The day of the national tragedy—my heart grows so heavy for the poor people killed by these most senseless acts. As I watch the coverage, I try to explain it to Wei, but I don't think he understands any of it. I'm not so sure how much any of us do.

September 16. As usual, Wei is so happy when I join him and Mr. L. for lunch. But tonight he's having trouble breathing.

September 17. They give him oxygen in the emergency room, and we all breathe easier. He's admitted to the hospital, and I finally go home, starving and exhausted. I phone and e-mail our children.

September 18. I bring a dish from a Chinese restaurant to Wei because I know he won't eat hospital food. The nurse tells me he's been very agitated. He touches my necklace and my clothes and asks me where I've been.

"There's no bed for me here. I had to go home to sleep."

"Let's go home now."

"You have to stay in the hospital for a while—"

"Let's go home now."

"—so you can get well enough to go home."

"Are you ready to go?"

His roommate's breathing machine is very disturbing. I talk to the nurse-in-charge, and Wei gets moved to a room down the hall.

September 20. He has congestive heart failure. He has to cut down on sodium. He's given a prescription and discharged.

September 21–25. At home, he's quiet and sleeps a lot. He refuses solid food. I don't think he can swallow it any more. He can't even finish a can of Ensure. He's going downhill very fast. It's tragic to watch him.

September 26. The doctor says soon he won't be able to swallow anything, and I'll have to decide if I want him fed through a stomach tube. Our children and I have discussed this eventuality. I tell him we want Wei to be comfortable. If anything can make him well again, we'll move Heaven and Earth to do it. Since his mind is gone and his body failing, our decision is to let him go peacefully, as long as he doesn't suffer.

September 27. Applesauce. Plain ice cream. Prayers. Sadness. He looks so thin.

September 28. Since Mr. L. can't speak English, I get a cell phone so he can call me if 9-1-1 needs to be called and I'm not there.

September 29. This morning I slowly give Wei apple cider and tell him I love him. I stroke his forehead. He smacks a kiss to me with his lips!

September 30. Ensure is now too thick for him to swallow. He manages a very small amount of ice cream, but it takes forever to go down.

October 1. I talk with the doctor about hospice at home and a sucking machine to relieve his discomfort from the matter accumulating in his throat.

October 2. Everything is sorrow in me. My loved one—the dearest and sweetest—is leaving me. There's this empty, awful feeling I can't describe.

October 3. Wei's eyes don't open all day. His fever is 102.1°. We put a sack of frozen peas in a towel on his forehead. The nurse says he's not in a coma and can hear me. I hold his hand and talk to him to let him know I'm there. I tell him he's going to a wonderful place, and I'll join him there some day.

October 4. I find him today with his eyes open wide! The nurse is surprised at how strong his vital signs are. I'm sure he's waiting for his children. They're on their way.

October 5. I sit by his bed most of the time, holding his hand and talking into his ear. I tell him to wait for the children and grandchildren. They'll be here tomorrow.

October 6. Our children and grandchildren arrive. Wei's breathing all right in the early afternoon, so I whisper in his ear, "I'm leaving you a little while for something important, but wait for me, OK? I want you to wait for me."

Eugene drives me around as I take care of things at the cemetery, chapel, and florist. When I get back, my love is waiting for me.

He's considerate to the end.

Fifteen minutes later, he takes a breath out of the corner of his mouth, pauses, then takes his last breath the same way. Our whole family is present. It's 3:05 PM. My devoted husband of over fifty-two years leaves this world for a better place, Heaven.

This is the most painful and saddest day of my life.

* * *

October 10. In the funeral chapel, the casket is opened for me. Wei looks so peaceful and elegant. I say good-bye and tell him that when we meet again, we'll never part, and we'll be together for eternity.

The day is absolutely beautiful, sunny, and cool—nothing but the best now for Wei.

October 20. Another perfect day for Wei's funeral celebration—on the altar, purple and yellow roses and baby's breath surround the beautiful cloisonné urn. Wei's photo is on one side, and the cross on the other. It all looks elegant, just the way Wei likes things to be.

Limos take us all to our favorite Chinese restaurant. I stand and thank God for his grace and love and for Wei. I tell everyone we're here to celebrate Wei's long, happy life with a long, happy banquet. Everyone seems to enjoy the fourteen-course dinner. Then three tiramisu cakes are brought out. The first is inscribed *Good-bye, Grandpa;* the second, *Farewell, Dad;* and the third, from me, is inscribed in Chinese, *See you again.*

October 21–November. One by one, everyone leaves. All of a sudden, my home is empty. It's so strange. How can I ever get used to this?

How I miss Wei. I wish we could have our old life back again.

Friends visit, family keeps in touch—all this love keeps me alive. Some days are even wonderful, even though I always feel that a piece of my heart is gone.

But some days are pure misery, and grief engulfs me. A call from Elaine will save me; a small prayer might give me hope or just the oblivion of sleep and the start of a new day. I keep the faith, and my faith keeps me. One day I awake and sing; the next I float aimlessly, without appetite for food or life. I miss Wei. I miss him everywhere I am.

November 13. Wei visits me in my dream! He is walking very slowly, but walking! I'm very happy. Maybe next time he'll even talk to me!

November 18. Elaine and Bob help set up my new computer so I can get to work on my book. Eugene calls every day just to make sure I'm all right. I have very loving and caring children.

November 24. After Thanksgiving, the children leave, and I know I am still grief-stricken. I look forward to the day my grief will fade. Meanwhile, I'm learning the computer and digesting my book ideas.

December. I dream I see Wei sitting on the smaller office chair, which he wheeled from his room into the hall. Just a short dream, but when I wake up, I feel that my grief is ever so slightly lighter.

Christmas is very lonely, as is our anniversary. Everywhere I go and everything I do reminds me of special times together. We spent so much time together because we enjoyed each other's company so much. As I watch the ball fall on New Year's Eve, I think: *My missing him so much is all I have of his company now.*

2002, January–May. My arthritis has searing flare-ups, the likes of which I haven't had for a number of years. I'm sure it's a delayed reaction to the exhausting last few years. I add Hara breathing, a Chinese technique of breathing from the *Hara*, or lower abdomen, to my morning exercise regimen. In Hara breathing, one gently touches the Hara area with one or both hands while deeply inhaling and exhaling with one's belly. Babies breathe like this naturally.

I also add turmeric capsules to my supplements to increase the efficiency of glucosamine and chondroitin. Despite the pain, all the chores, messy work, sleepless nights, goofed-up emergencies, and unpleasant events of the last few years seem to have vanished from my mind. I barely remember them, let alone the details. Now only fond memories of Wei come to me. It's like forgetting the pain of childbirth once your beautiful baby is put in your arms.

Still, piercing sadness marks many of my days, usually accompanied by joint pain. Nevertheless, the tide rolls in and the tide rolls out. Wei continues to visit me in my dreams. Some I remember; others just barely, if at all. In one dream, Wei comes walking toward me with a big smile. He looks ecstatic. I am sure this means he is happy where he is, just as I told him he would be. When I tell this dream to my son, he says, "See? He's coming to say, 'You were right again!'" The next day my arthritic condition starts improving dramatically.

May 21. I dream Wei and I are young again, shining with health, going about our normal life. He's carrying everything I bought, sitting some place, waiting for me.

CHAPTER 12

PAIN AND VICTORY: THE CONTINUING STORY

2002–2003. I miss my dear husband a great deal. When I listen to music, I think of him and miss him. When I eat in the restaurant, I think of him and miss him. When I walk on the street, I think of him and I miss him. We were always together, like Siamese twins. I know in my heart I will feel the same way the rest of my life, until we are together again.

But life goes on, the highs and the lows. We share happiness with those who are glad and sadness with those who grieve. My spirit soars when Tarryn graduates from high school with many honors and falls when two close friends die within seven months of Wei. I thank God for days when my RA behaves and cling to him more closely when it doesn't.

A new rheumatologist finds me so healthy and my medicine so minimal that he tells me I don't have to see him again. I am in good shape for another major operation—elbow replacement surgery.

My elbows give me a lot of trouble. The left gives me sharp pain at certain angles, and the right one is too weak to use much. Doctor E. tells me the only solutions are either drugs to relieve the pain or elbow replacement surgery. The surgery, he says, is a two-hour procedure with a hospital stay of two days and a six-week recovery. This is much better than what my research has led me to believe, but also much better than what it actually turns out to be.

Only a local anesthetic will be used, he says, and blood clots won't be a worry. Infection, as usual, is always a danger, and he'll take great pains to avoid it.

If he doesn't, the "great pains" will be mine. Infection in a prosthesis is a notoriously hard plague to scour away completely. And if it's not completely removed, it's as bad as not being treated at all.

Speaking of pain, at our next meeting, Dr. E. tells me there will be lots of it. I've heard that before! As you might have guessed, having lots of experience with it doesn't make it hurt less. He assures me, however, that after surgery my right elbow will be 100 percent mobile. Since I am right-handed, this will relieve my pain-riddled left elbow, and it probably won't need surgery. He revises his estimate of recovery time to three months.

I arrange for physical therapy three times a week, and for my cleaning lady to work full-time the week after surgery. I cook some meals for when I come home, have a shower and massage, and arrive early at the hospital. My room's not ready. I wait forever for a hospital gown and have to walk in my stocking feet a long way on the hard floor, which hurts my feet. I tell the anesthesiologist I'm ultrasensitive to morphine, and before I know it I'm dead to the world—so much for a local anesthetic.

Are these normal hospital indignities or warning signs?

After I wake up, there's another long delay before they can wheel me to my room from recovery. "Anything to eat?" I ask. They tell me the kitchen is closed. "What?" They finally rustle me up a vegetable sandwich, which I devour. At this point, I'm so hungry I could eat a slipper.

I get all set to fall sleep, and I'm suddenly struck by lightning bolts of pain. *From where?* I look up and see a big heavy blimp floating above me. Then more pain—like a sharp knife cutting my fingers—and I realize the blimp above me is my arm elevated on a rack. I'm connected to that arm, and the huge nerve that controls all its fingers is sending out roaring five-alarm fires. I push the button for pain medicine, and they give me morphine.

It is just what I warned them not to give me.

I start vomiting repeatedly, soiling everything. I can't eat anything for the next three days and have to stay in this clown palace a day longer than expected—dizzy, weak, headachy, and unable to sleep more than two hours a stretch. They give me a different pain medication without telling me what it is. I have a bad reaction to it as well.

Finally, they give me what I ask for: Tylenol 3, but it only lasts three hours. The nurse says I have to wait another hour before getting more. Does she think she's getting revenge because I didn't like her other offerings? Each second seems like a lifetime of pain. The nurse returns with the second dosage long after the fourth hour. Sadists must like to work in hospitals. This Tylenol takes care of my pain, and I don't need any more.

I go home the next day. Elaine is there to help me. I start therapy that week. In three weeks, my splint is taken off, but soon I notice the dressing is spotting. My doctor takes one look at it and says, "Infection." This is bad news—very bad news.

Right back to the hospital to see infectious disease specialists and get blood cultures: it's *Staphylococcus aureus.* I have to take intravenous antibiotics every six hours for two weeks. The results: It only inhibits and doesn't kill the bacteria. I have to start over. Six weeks of another antibiotic.

I'm in the thick of the most devastating nightmare of my life. Twenty days in the hospital, three more surgeries to flush the metal prosthesis of the staph. They tell me I'm lucky it worked after only three times.

Then I have intravenous antibiotics in a nursing facility. The food is horrible—I lose my appetite. I get even weaker. My temperature reaches a 103°. I have to go back to the hospital. Is the infection in my intravenous lines?

They decide to take the line out from the right side and put a new line in the left side. Just a half hour, they say. My head is pushed to the side and immobilized on a cold plastic pillow for over an hour. The procedure is torturous, and they find no infection in the old line! Moreover, the uncomfortable position puts my jaw out of alignment (a condition known as TMJ), so there goes any chance of chewing. I'm losing quite a bit of weight, and I don't have that much to start with.

Eight more days in the hospital, and they finally pronounce, "No infection." I have to stay in two more weeks just to make sure!

Dear Lord, should I stay in this house-of-pain hospital, return to the indifferent nursing facility, or go home to an uninsured medical set-up?

Dear Anita, Go home!

So I get on the phone, make the arrangements, and shell out the money. The Lord's advice, as might be expected, works out all for the good. I go home.

Elaine is a godsend again. She learns how to give me the intravenous treatments every six hours and adjusts her sleeping schedule. I'm almost paralyzed with weakness from the medicine, but she watches over me like my own Florence Nightingale.

Finally, my day of liberation arrives, and the treatments end. I'm still very dizzy and staggering, and I'm worried about taking a disastrous fall. A hematologist starts giving me Procrit injections and says I might need three months to fully recover.

It only takes me four weeks. The doctors all want to know the secret of my speedy recuperative powers. My answer: God is good, and I try to take care of my body and soul as best I can.

I pray my thanks and start eating again to regain my health and strength. Elaine has been with me for more than three months. Bless her and her husband, Bob, who has used this time to learn the valuable skills of cooking and doing laundry! My elbow is now a thing of marvelous, elastic utility, and there are days I want to shout to the world how great I feel.

I start my regular dietary supplements: the most important ones first, adding the others as my appetite increases. I take public transportation, go to the health food store, see a movie, tidy the books, and catch up on my housekeeping.

2002, October 6. A year after Wei's passing, some friends and I add flowers to the ones already in his "neighborhood" at the cemetery. This honorable neighborhood includes my parents and brother, and my sister and brother-in-law. Afterward we have a delicious lunch in Chinatown, where Wei and I used to go so often. It's a sad, sweet day.

Each day I try to walk fifteen to twenty blocks, rest, have a massage, listen to music, and get back to writing this book. Reading my diaries gives me joy as well as sadness. My health keeps gradually improving. Days of sustained pleasure are given to me that I haven't felt in over fifty-two years. Thank you, Source of All.

I give a dinner party for all the kind friends who were most caring during my time in the hospital and during my recuperation. I give a little speech before the meal thanking each one, with a special mention of my devoted daughter and her husband. Everyone loves the dinner and enjoys each other even more than the food.

* * *

The great poet Emily Dickinson wrote, "After great pain, a formal feeling comes." I believe everything happens for a reason. My nightmare with the infection, as with all the pain in my life, has made me stronger. My faith deepens.

To this day my arthritic condition continues to improve. Weather doesn't affect my joints anymore. I am still a little lonely, but I enjoy the peace and have a vibrant life. When my heart aches, I know Wei is there, still with me. Writing these pages has turned into a pleasure, as I have reflected in tranquility on a rich life surrounded by beautiful music and a world of friends.

My only hope, dear reader, is that this book imparts to you something of the goodness I've been given. My deepest prayer is that this account of my lifelong dealings with rheumatoid arthritis will reach many of my fellow victims and be of help.

CHAPTER 13

SELF-HELP

No cure has yet been found for rheumatoid arthritis, despite years of research and development. We need medical doctors to diagnose, evaluate, and treat our RA conditions. However, many new drugs can help relieve joint pain and delay deformation. Unfortunately, as with any other drugs, there are side effects, and the new drugs are extremely expensive. Over the years, I have found that self-help has played a major role in my general health and reducing joint discomforts, with the result that my life is more comfortable and pleasant. There are many facets to what I have been doing to achieve this unheard-of success.

The first thing to remember is that rest is very important. Pain takes a lot out of our bodies. We need to rest as much as possible. I only wish I could have done this earlier so that I would have reached my goal sooner.

I keep away from any food that has preservatives, additives, and other artificial ingredients. I use products from health food stores, particularly, vegetables and fruits that are organically grown. Organic produce tastes better and fresher and is more nutritious.

I also eliminate all citrus fruits and nightshade vegetables. Nightshade vegetables include green and red bell peppers, tomatoes, eggplants, and white potatoes.

I cook with all-natural ingredients, and when I eat out I make sure that the dishes are free of monosodium glutamate (MSG), a flavor enhancer often used in Chinese restaurants. I request that the dishes be cooked without MSG, with less oil and less salt, and without ready-made sauces. Keep away from very spicy dishes. Steamed dishes are good.

I avoid refined sugar and flour. I use raw honey sparingly as a sweetener and eat foods made with whole wheat, rye, oats, and other whole grains. Fruits are usually served as dessert. I eat desserts made with white sugar and white flour only once in a blue moon.

I also eat only brown rice and dry cereal without preservatives and lightly sweetened with only fruit juice. Rolled oats and brown Cream of Wheat are my hot cereals. A combination of nuts, hot cereal, fruits, and rice milk makes a tasty, nutritious, and hearty breakfast. I eat this breakfast three or four times a week. On other days, I have eggs and toast or cold cereal. For protein, I mainly eat fish and other seafood, chicken, and turkey. I do not eat red meat, such as beef, lamb, and pork.

I do not drink coffee, tea, or other beverages containing caffeine. Instead, I drink herbal teas, decaffeinated teas, seltzer water, spring water, filtered water, and rice milk. (Cow's milk is not agreeable to me.) I have apple juice but not every day. All sodas are eliminated in my diet because of their sugar, caffeine, and artificial ingredients.

Food allergens play a part in arthritis. Allergies can vary a lot from person to person. To find out what you are allergic to is not difficult, but it takes patience. You need to eliminate each suspected food one by one for a week or so. If eliminating the food improves your condition, you should avoid that food.

Besides the good and healthy foods I consume, I also take many dietary supplements. Below I list the ones that I have been taking for a number of years that I have found to be very beneficial to my arthritic condition and overall health:

1. The basic antioxidant vitamins: vitamin C, vitamin E, beta-carotene, and selenium (For the vitamin C, I prefer Ester-C because it contains no acid.)
2. Aloe Vera capsules
3. Vitamin B-100 complex, time-released
4. Liquid calcium gel caps with vitamin D, taken together with magnesium in a 2-to-1 ratio (So, if you take 500 mg of calcium, you should also take 250 mg of magnesium.)
5. Omega-3 gel caps containing EPA (eicosa-pentaenoic acid) and DHA (docosahexaenoic acid)
6. Evening primrose oil
7. Glucosamine and chondroitin
8. MSM (methylsulfonylmethane)
9. Shark cartilage
10. Lutein and bilberry (for eye health)
11. Multi-vitamin with minerals

12. Citrus bioflavonoid
13. Alfalfa tablets

I try out new supplements one at a time and watch for at least a few weeks to see if a particular supplement helps my arthritis. If the supplement helps, it is put into my dietary supplement regimen. If it does not help, I discontinue taking it. After some new discoveries, I recently added:

14. Turmeric extract capsule with 95% of curcumin, which makes glucosamine and chondroitin more effective (Curcumin can only be found in turmeric capsules.)
15. Sun chlorella
16. Cordyceps
17. Lycopene

In addition to eating nutritious foods and taking dietary supplements, we rheumatoid arthritics can make other aspects of our daily lives more pleasant.

For instance, consider the pillows on which we sleep. I have tried many kinds of pillows and find that a soft pillow is most suitable for me. It helps my neck and shoulders. For me, the pillow is soft enough when it can be folded together lengthwise. I am allergic to down, so I use a polyester-filled pillow, which is inexpensive and just as soft as a down pillow. For rheumatoid arthritis, it's worth the trouble to find the perfect pillow.

The mattress is important too. We should try out many mattresses in the store to find the most comfortable one. (I like a firm mattress.) To keep the mattress in good condition, I have it turned every few months, changing the head and feet positions or flipping the mattress over completely. Mattresses should be replaced with new ones every eight to ten years. We spend approximately one-third of our lives in bed, so comfort and support are very important to us all.

Clothes should be comfortable and never tight enough to block circulation. Shoes, in my opinion, are the most important pieces of clothing. Shoes have to support the feet, which support the weight of the whole body. When standing or walking, shoes must fit like a natural part of the feet. They should allow room for the toes to spread. The wrong pair of shoes can cause fatigue and can cause pain in the ankles, knees, hips, and back. Shoes with rubber soles provide better cushioning than ones with hard leather soles. High heels are bad. Years ago I learned from an orthopedic shoe specialist the proper way to walk: lift the foot, step down on the heel first, and then step on the toes. Walking like this puts a spring in my step!

We should keep our joints warm, especially while we are sleeping (when our circulation slows down) and at all times in the winter. Many kinds of knee, leg, elbow, and arm warmers are available. I knit my own with a rib stitch. My homemade warmers fit better than the commercial ones I initially bought. I also wear socks to bed. However, when a joint is inflamed, we need to get the swelling down. A bag of frozen peas makes a great ice pack, since it can be molded to fit the shape of the joint. I always keep a pack of peas (get the cheapest one) in my freezer. Wrap a towel over the bag of peas before applying it to the swollen joint.

Neck pain is very common and can be persistent. The neck has to support not only the heavy weight of the head but also its motion—nodding, turning, and tilting. Besides the neck exercises I do every day to strengthen the muscles, I rest my neck whenever I can. When I use my computer, I make sure that I have a CD playing. When the music stops, it reminds me that it is time to get up to rest my eyes, my neck, and my shoulders. While I'm watching television, I also prop a small pillow on the back of the sofa on which to rest my neck and head.

Sitting for a long time may result in stiffness. It is best not to sit for more than forty-five minutes straight. Periodically getting up out of your seat and moving about will help to avoid discomfort. In addition, while you are seated, do not keep your legs crossed at the knees for periods longer than ten minutes (Fig. 1).

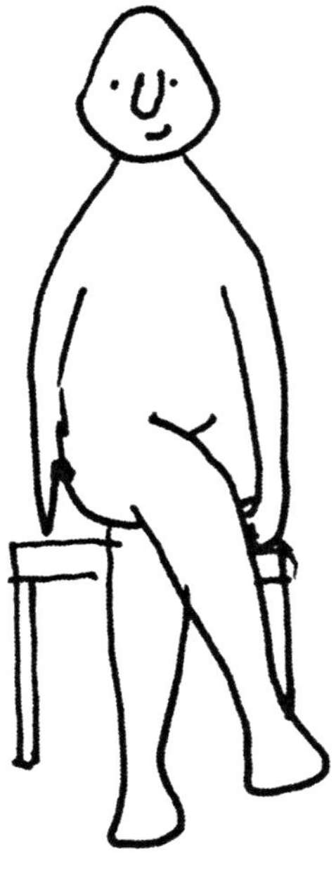

Figure 1. Do not sit with crossed legs for long periods.

In our daily life, stress is unavoidable. We can try to avoid or combat some of these stresses, however. One such way is by deep breathing. The trick is to inhale for one count, then exhale for three counts: one count in, and one, two, three counts out. Try to relax every muscle in your body when exhaling. I learned this technique from a physician years ago. It works!

As I have done since 1959, I also use an electric thermo-massage pad once or, if time permits, twice a day to relax my body as I listen to music. Music banishes stress and lifts the spirits. In my opinion, music is the best gift from God. I have a large collection of classical, inspirational, instrumental, and vocal music. I like to sing along with and dance to the music. When my late husband was suffering from Alzheimer's disease, I put on lively music and encouraged him to dance with me. It was therapeutic for both of us. Now that I have lost my dear partner, although it may sound crazy, I dance solo at times. Besides, dancing is very good exercise.

As for exercise, there is no doubt that regular physical exercise helps reduce stress and is necessary for good health. Chapter 14 contains information on effortless exercises for arthritics to strengthen our muscles and joints and improve our mobility.

Over the years, I have figured out ways and found devices that make daily life much easier and more comfortable, reduce frustration, and increase independence. Listed below are the techniques and helpful devices I use. It does no harm to give them a try.

Day-to-Day Living

1. Use a small set of pliers to turn switches. Wrap the teeth of the pliers with masking tape in order to avoid scratching the surface of the switch.
2. To turn a lock, use a large serving fork (Figs. 2–4).

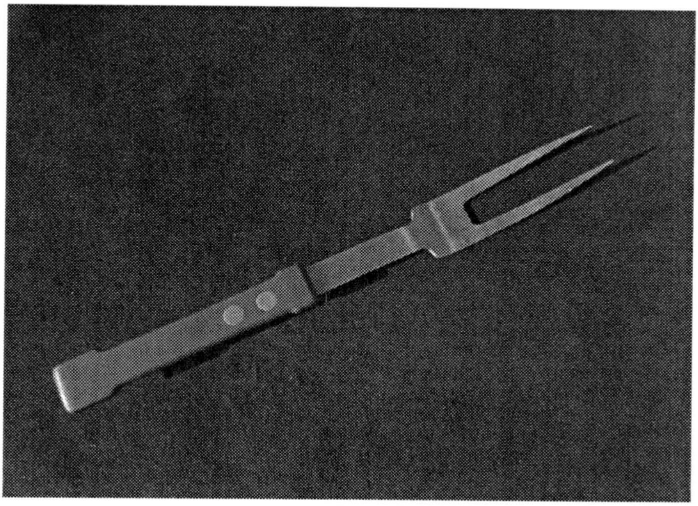

Figure 2. Large serving fork.

Figure 3. Place a large fork on the lock's knob.

Figure 4. Rotate the large fork to turn the lock.

3. To turn a key, use a small, sturdy fork (Figs. 5–7).

Figure 5. Small fork.

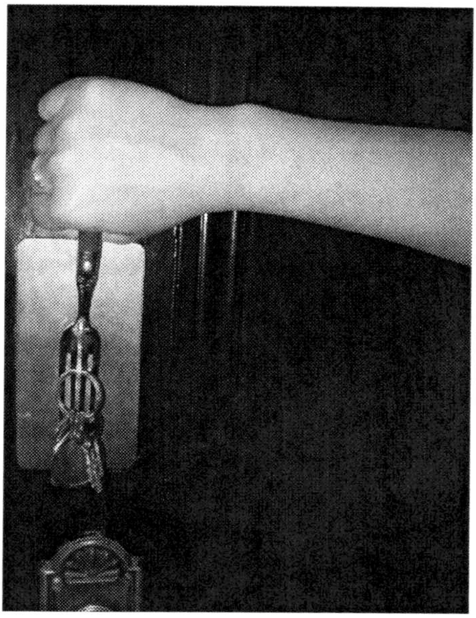

Figure 6. Slip the key between two of the tines of the fork.

Figure 7. Rotate the fork to turn the key.

4. If an item is too heavy for one hand, use two hands.
5. Use a magnet to pick up pins and needles easily.
6. If something is difficult to pull, try pushing it from the other end!
7. When loading a shopping cart, be sure to pack the items in bags with handles and put the bags into the shopping cart one at a time. This makes unloading the cart easier because the bags are not too heavy to lift. Another way to get the packages out of the shopping cart is to lay the back of the shopping cart on the floor, tilt the bottom up, and let the packages slide out.
8. Waiting in line in the post office or any other place can be stressful. When I'm in this situation, looking back and seeing that there is a long line behind me makes me feel better.
9. When I cannot reach something, I use a backscratcher to pull the object closer to me. Every time I've gone to the hospital for surgery, I've packed a backscratcher to reach my slippers, which usually got scattered when the room was cleaned.
10. Use electrical versions of devices whenever possible, such as can openers, beaters, toothbrushes, and razors.

11. Opening an envelope is frustrating if the card or letter fits snugly in the envelope. Slitting the top and also an inch or so along the sides of the envelope will make more room for sliding the contents out.
12. I always carry a pair of small scissors in my handbag to cut open single-serve tea bag packages or other similar packets. When I cut the tea bag packet, I cut the top with a curve because many times I find that the tag of the tea bag is stuck at the top. Then I can slip the scissors next to the tea bag in the cut opening and finish cutting open the packet.
13. A tea- or coffeepot can be difficult to lift by the handle with one hand. Instead, I tilt my cup under the spout with one hand and tilt the pot by the handle with the other hand to pour. This way I can get at least half of a cup without asking for assistance or getting burned. Alternatively, I can move the pot to the edge of the table and position it to pour the tea into a cup that I hold with the other hand just beyond the edge of the table and a little lower than the pot.
14. When I open a bag, I cut a corner or slit large enough to pour some of the contents out. If the bag contains food, any food left in the bag will stay fresher longer with the smaller opening.
15. I use plastic clothespins to reseal opened bags. To press the pin open with just a thumb and forefinger is difficult for a weak hand. Instead, I place the pin on the edge of a table (or any other stable flat surface), press the pin open with my entire hand, and stick the folded opening of the bag into the clothespin.
16. If your knees bother you, spread your legs apart a little bit. This technique makes sitting down, getting up, or bending down easier.

Food Preparation

1. Use good quality knives to reduce the stress caused by blunt knives.
2. Cutting carrots and other vegetables is often hard on hands, so I cook the vegetable first, usually in the microwave. If the entire piece is too big to fit, I cut it in half and then cook it. Once the vegetable is soft, it can be cut into small pieces. Sometimes a knife is not necessary, and the vegetable slices easily with just a plastic utensil. This method also works well for zucchinis.
3. When cutting round vegetables, such as cucumbers and zucchinis, use one hand to rotate the vegetable slowly beneath the knife blade as the other hand cuts.

4. When scraping the skins off round vegetables, such as carrots and zucchinis, I find it easier to stand the vegetable on its end and scrape down vertically.
5. When slicing leafy vegetables, such as lettuce and cabbage, I find it easier to cut on the inner side of the leaf. It takes less effort to start cutting through the inside surface since the edges stick up off the cutting board (Figs. 8–9).

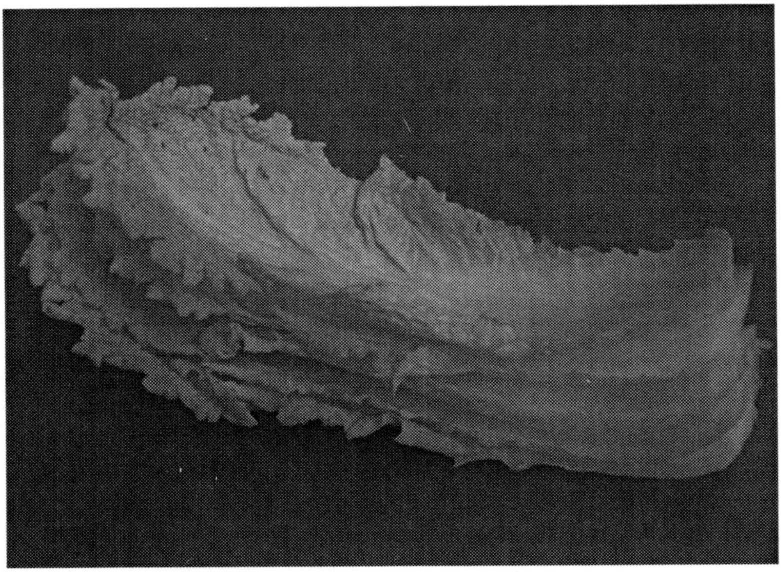

Figure 8. Leafy vegetable with inner side up.

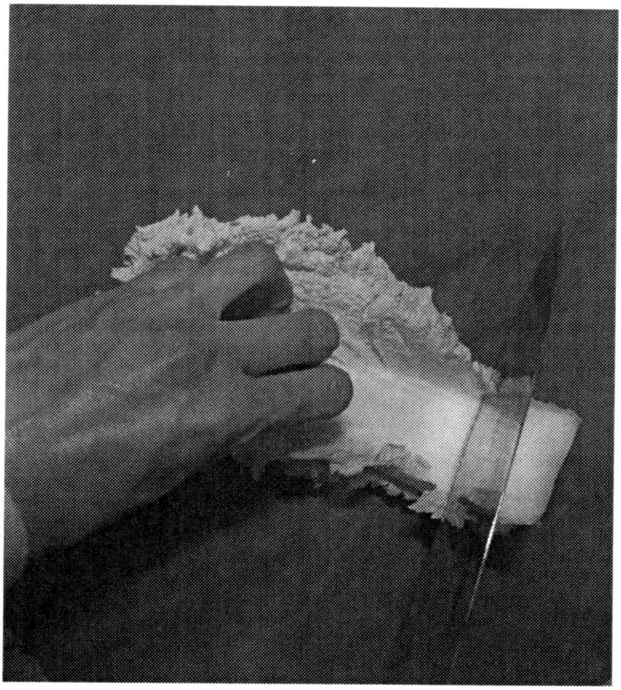

Figure 9. Slice through the inner side of leafy vegetables.

6. Squeezing lemon juice is difficult for weak hands. First quarter the lemon lengthwise, then cut the center parts out and remove the seeds. With clean thumbs, scrape between the skins of each section to extract the juice. I get more juice this way than by squeezing. If I do not need the pulp, I use a small strainer to catch the pulp. Typically, I use the pulp and juice together to marinate chicken or fish. (I did not use lemons for many years because of the acid content. However, since I feel much better now, I occasionally use lemons.)
7. If a teakettle is too heavy to handle when it is full, fill it only halfway with water. Or instead, use a small pot to boil water. A single cup of water can be boiled in the microwave, as well.

Personal Care

1. I like to wash my face with a face towel. At times, when the towel is soaked with water, it is too heavy for me to wring out. I fold the wet towel in two,

put it flat on the dry side of the basin, and rub the water out. If my hands are very weak or painful, I use a sponge to clean my face. It is easier to squeeze a wet sponge than a wet face towel.

2. To dry my back after bathing, I use a towel that I modified for easier use. I bought the thinnest hand towel I could find and folded it in half lengthwise. I then sewed each of the two ends with bias tape to make loops big enough for my hands to fit through comfortably and use as straps for pulling the towel across my back (Fig. 10). I also dry my back by using a regular bath towel that I wrap around my back and hold in front with a diagonal corner in each hand. I then move my covered elbows back and forth to slide the towel across my back. The towel can be shifted lower or higher to reach other back parts.

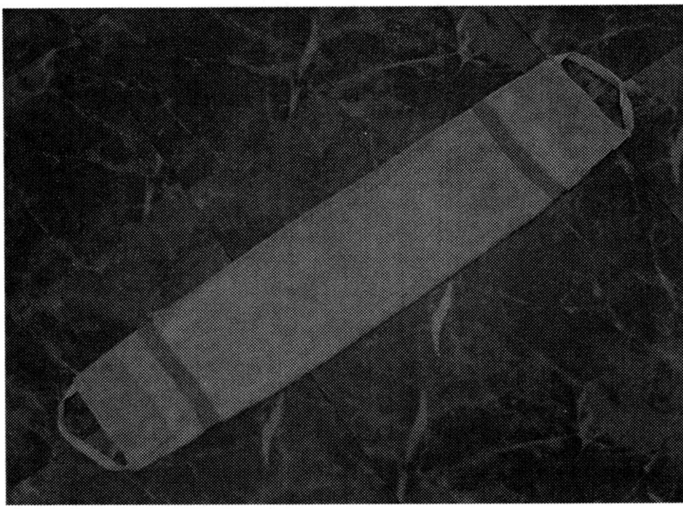

Figure 10. Modified towel for drying off after bathing.

3. To clean my back in the shower, I use soap with a long and flexible store-bought back scrubber.

4. When taking off socks or pants is too much work for my hands, a plastic shoehorn comes in handy. I push the sock down to my ankle, place the shoehorn inside the heel, and slide the sock off. This method works for taking off tight pants too.

5. For ladies who have difficulty hooking a brassiere in the back, I have a convenient trick. I turn the brassiere upside down and inside out and put it around my torso with the hooks in the front. After I put the hooks together, I just slide the hooked area around to my back and pull the straps over my arms to complete putting on the brassiere. There is also a wide selection of front-closing brassieres on the market.
6. Removing a pullover top is simple if I bend my head down, put my chin and part of my face in the collar opening, and pull the back of the collar over my head. I learned this from watching Westerns! Cowhands remove their sweat-soaked shirts in this way. In fact, a button-down shirt can be treated like a pullover. I leave a couple of the top buttons unbuttoned to make enough room for my head to go through. Doing this also saves me the trouble of doing and undoing the whole line of buttons each time I want to put on or take off the shirt.
7. Many arthritics have lower back problems. To help this, I place a small, flat pillow under my lower back and a leg lift (Fig. 11) under my legs when I sleep. The leg lift eases pressure on the lower back and increases circulation. There are also stretching exercises that help me enormously. The stretches are detailed in Chapter 14.

Figure 11. Leg lift.

In general, we must have patience, patience, and more patience to cope with our arthritic condition. We must allow ourselves ample time to do even the simplest things. Rushing only creates unnecessary stress and frustration. I always give myself plenty of time to get ready for dinner parties or other events with friends. I would rather be early than late.

A feeling of helplessness and defeat diminishes our chance of improvement. I regularly pray for divine guidance. Faith in God is a miracle drug. It gives results! We all have faith in varying degrees. Faith grows if we use it, and it can grow without bounds. We must also have faith in ourselves and take responsibility for our lives. We should be our own day-to-day arthritis doctors and monitor our conditions. Don't let arthritis get control of us; get control of our arthritis.

I treat rheumatoid arthritis as if it's an archenemy that wants to disable me and steal my independence. With any wisdom God gives me, I think of all kinds of ways and find various devices to aid me in my daily life. Every time I succeed, I feel victorious because I have won a battle. I can remain independent. We arthritics must have a positive attitude in everything we do. We must have tenacity and self-discipline to fight this devastating disease. These traits are good for everyone, with or without arthritis.

I tell my children that fear and worry are poisons. Don't touch them. They do not help in any situation. Instead, they create misery and shorten lives.

I picture myself as an inflated ball. When I get hit, I bounce. The harder I get hit, the higher I bounce.

We also should be *consistent* in whatever we do that is good for us, whether it is exercise, diet, or dietary supplement intake. Consistency produces unbelievable results.

I feel it's our lifetime mission to get better and better in our arthritic condition. I have succeeded by doing what I have written in this book. I still keep learning of the newest discoveries that can improve my life. I always look for any health-related news on television or in print (see Appendix 1), and I evaluate each new piece of information with an open mind. So far, I have led an independent life. I can do practically everything people without arthritis can do. In fact, there are days I want to shout to the world how great I feel! Such days come to me more and more frequently now.

It is my fervent prayer that they come more and more frequently to you too.

CHAPTER 14

EXERCISE

Even those who have no serious health problems need exercise to stay healthy. This doesn't necessarily mean we have to get on the floor and move around vigorously like we often see on television. We arthritics can modify our exercises so they don't aggravate troublesome joints.

In this chapter, I describe (with illustrations) the exercises I do, some every day and some often. These exercises have helped me stay mobile. I am sure they will help anyone willing to give them a try. However, before you start any exercise regimen, please consult your physician. Your physician may want you to see a physical therapist, who will evaluate your particular condition and needs and recommend specific exercises.

I have learned that even arthritics can make their joints and muscles more mobile through exercise, and it definitely improves our general health. No matter how little exercise you are able to do, some is better than none. When we are in pain, it is tempting to lead a sedentary life. Such a life, however, is detrimental to our health and agitates arthritis problems.

Of course we should not exercise inflamed joints. My experience is that not all my joints are inflamed at one time. The inflammation roams to different joints on different days. There are always some joints I can exercise. (And remember, a bag of frozen peas wrapped in a towel and applied to the joint reduces inflammation.) Some exercises can even be done while sitting and watching television. Walking is always excellent, even with a walker or cane, or dancing, if you prefer. The main thing is to stop sitting and get moving!

EXERCISE INSTRUCTIONS

I learned some of the following exercises during my various hospital stays. Most of the exercises were taught to me by a professional therapist, who came to my home to show me how to keep fit from head to toe. Start doing exercises at a comfortable rate and then gradually increase the repetitions.

I. Hail That Cab

(upper stretch)

1. Stand with your feet shoulder-width apart.
2. Stretch one arm up diagonally in front of your face and hold for five seconds.
3. Bring your arm back down.
4. Do the same stretch with the other arm.

Do ten repetitions, two times per day.

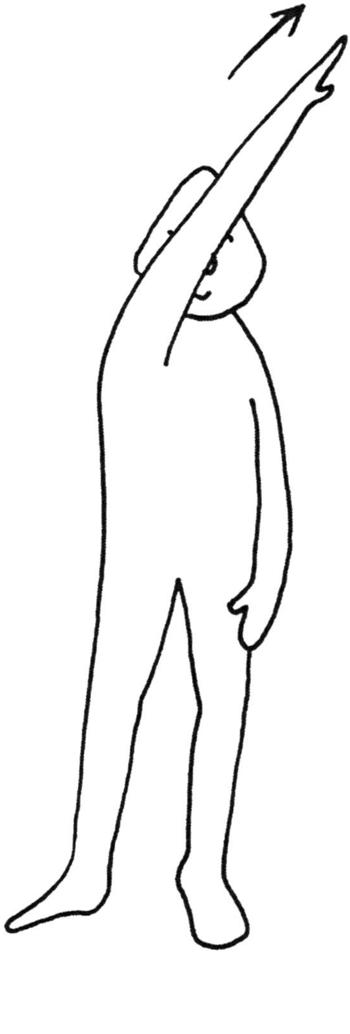

II. I Don't Know

(shoulder shrugs)

1. Lift your shoulders up toward the sky.
2. Push your shoulders down toward the floor.
3. Bring your shoulders back to the starting position.

Do ten repetitions, two times per day.

III. Arm Yourself, Part 1

(arm pull across body)

1. Secure one end of an exercise band or tubing around a sturdy post or in a doorjamb about hip-height.
2. Stand with one side of your body facing the post or door. Grasp the band or tubing with the hand farthest from the post or door and let this arm lay across your body.
3. Slowly pull the band or tubing across the front of your body and out to the side.
4. Slowly return to the starting position.

Do ten repetitions with each arm per set, two sets per day.

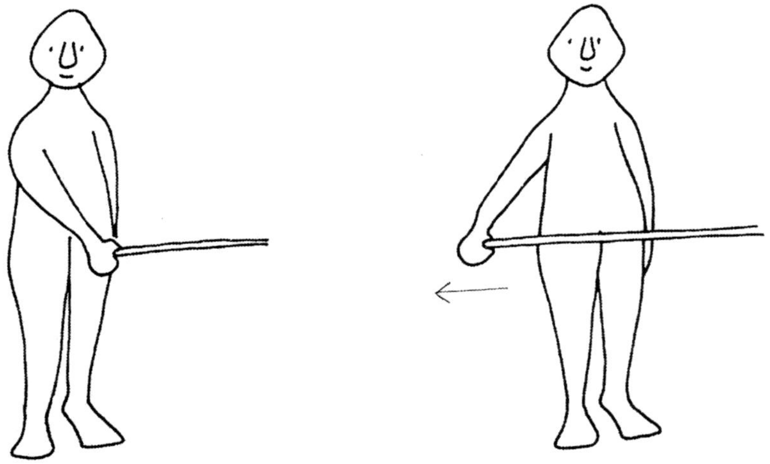

IV. Arm Yourself, Part 2

(arm rotation)

1. Secure one end of an exercise band or tubing around a sturdy post or in a doorjamb about waist-high above the floor.
2. Stand with one side of your body toward the post or door. Grasp the band or tubing with the hand farthest from the post or door. Keep your elbow at your side and your arm across your body.
3. Slowly rotate your arm outward so that it points away from your body. Make sure to keep your forearm parallel to the floor during the motion.
4. Slowly return to the starting position.

Do ten repetitions with each arm per set, two sets per day.

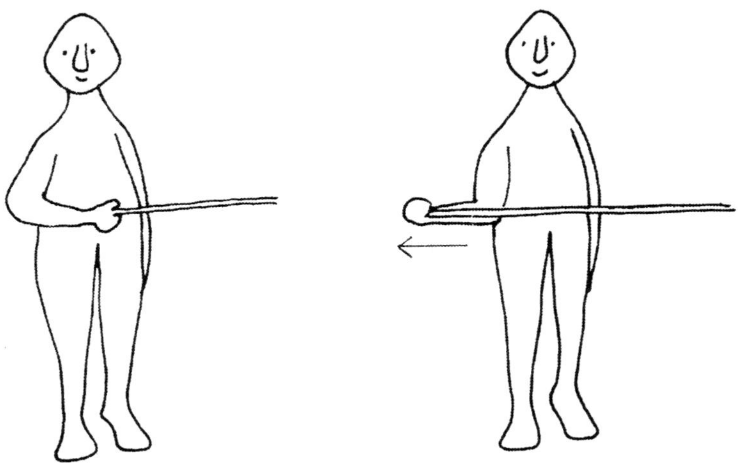

V. Arm Yourself, Part 3

(elbow flexes)

1. While seated, hold one end of an exercise band or tubing under your foot and bring the band or tubing up along the outer side of your leg.
2. With the hand on the same side of your body, grasp the free end of the band or tubing.
3. Slowly pull the band or tubing up toward you as you curl your arm. Make sure to keep your elbow close to your side.
4. Slowly lower your forearm to the starting position.

Do ten repetitions with each arm per set, two sets per day.

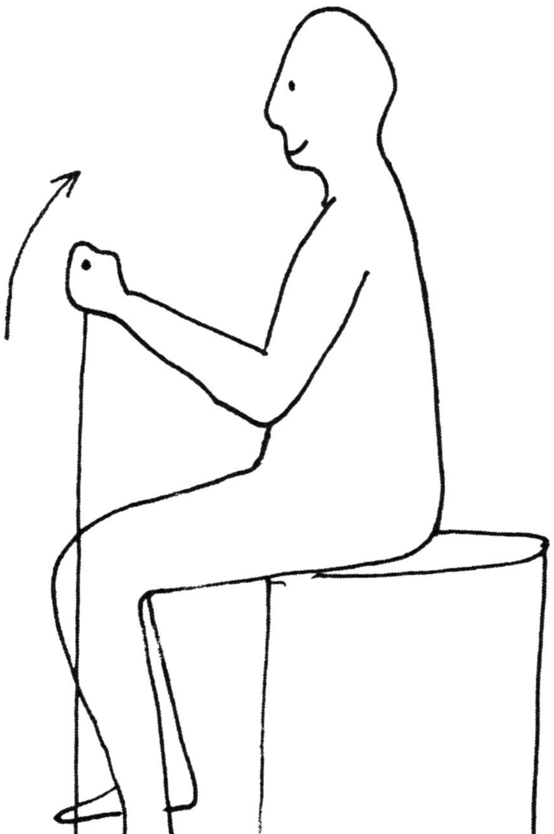

VI. Arm Yourself, Part 4

(elbow extensions)

1. Secure one end of an exercise band or tubing around a sturdy post or in a doorjamb about shoulder-height above the floor when seated.
2. Sit with your back to the post or door. Grasp the free end of the band or tubing with one hand and hold it just above your shoulder with your elbow bent.
3. Slowly straighten your elbow so that your arm is pointing forward.
4. Slowly return to the starting position.

Do ten repetitions with each arm per set, two sets per day.

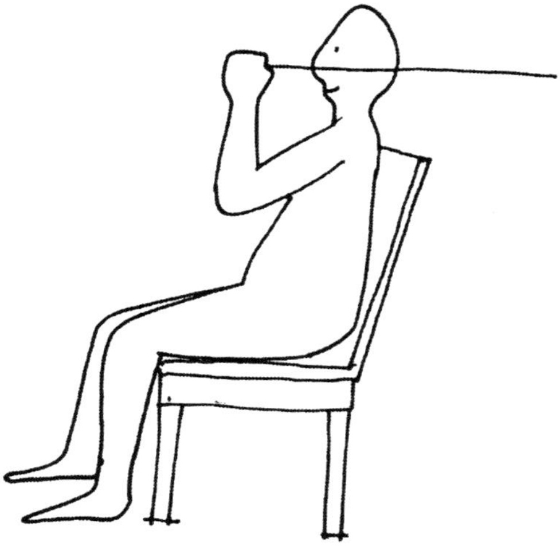

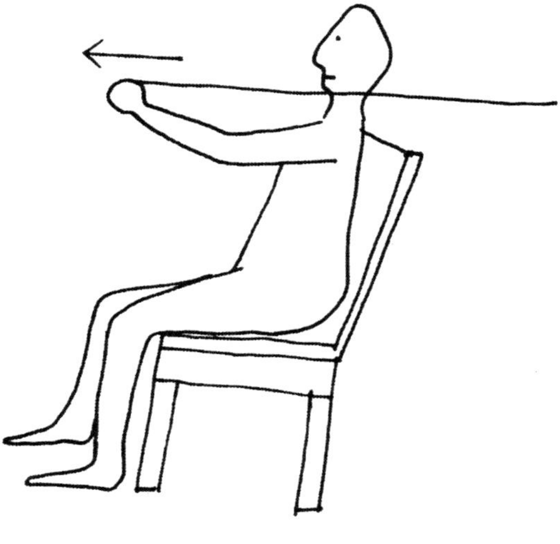

VII. Scrap That Paper

(paper crumple)

1. Place your palm on a sheet of tissue paper on a flat surface.
2. While keeping the heel of your hand touching the surface, crumple the tissue up into a ball.

Do ten repetitions for each hand per set, two sets per session, two sessions per day.

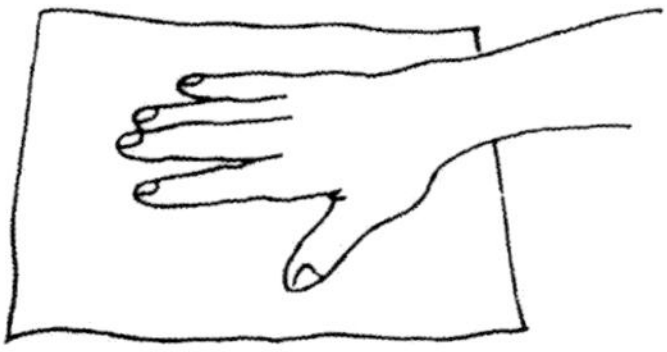

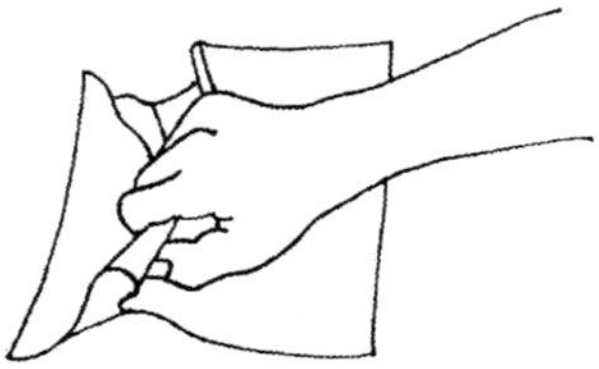

VIII. Step Up & Swing

(knee lift with leg extension)

1. Get a chair for support.
2. Holding on to the chair, lift one knee toward your chest.
3. Straighten your leg out and swing it back and forth for five seconds.
4. Now do the same sequence with the other leg.

Do ten repetitions, two times per day.

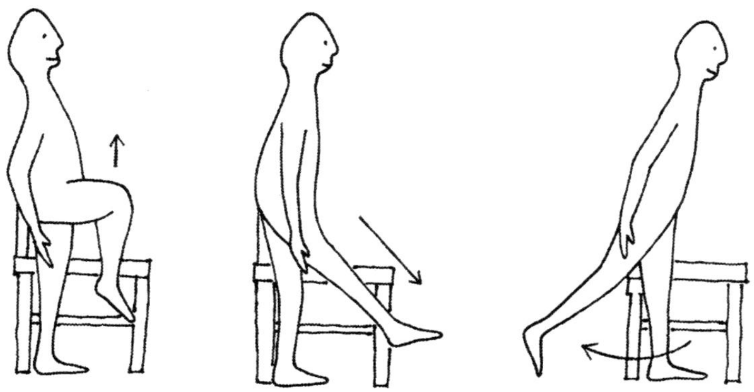

IX. Do the Swing Step, Part 1

(leg pull outward)

1. Secure one end of an exercise band or tubing close to the floor around a sturdy post or in a doorjamb.
2. Secure the other end of the band or tubing around the ankle area of one leg.
3. Stand so that the side of your body with the free leg faces the post or door. Make sure there is some tension in the band.
4. Keeping your banded leg straight, slowly pull the band or tubing out to the side and then back to the starting position.

Do ten repetitions with each leg, two times per day.

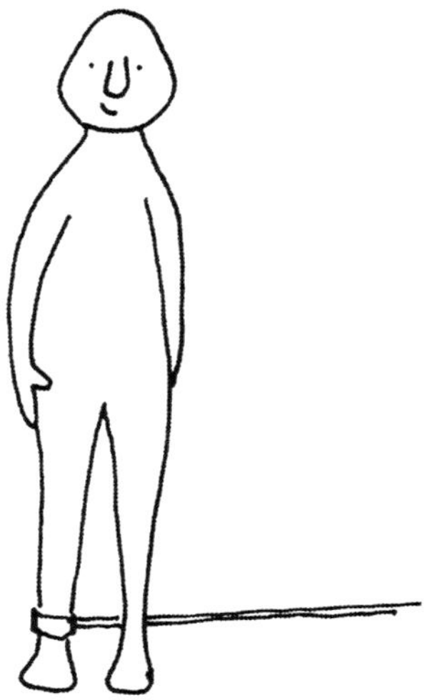

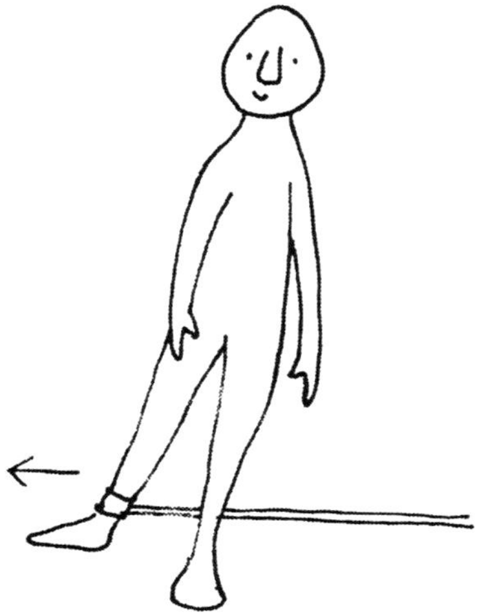

X. Do the Swing Step, Part 2

(leg pull across front)

1. Secure one end of an exercise band or tubing close to the floor around a sturdy post or in a doorjamb.
2. Secure the other end of the band or tubing around the ankle area of one leg.
3. Stand so that the side of your body with the banded leg faces the post or door. Hold the post or the doorframe with the closest arm for support.
4. Keeping your banded leg straight, slowly pull the band or tubing across the front of the other leg and then back to the starting position.

Do ten repetitions with each leg, two times per day.

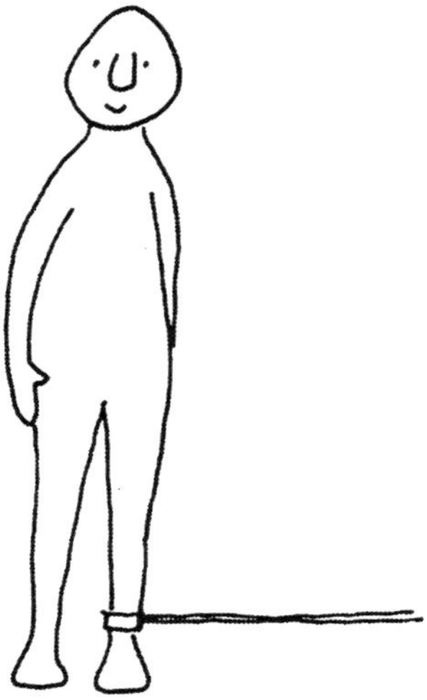

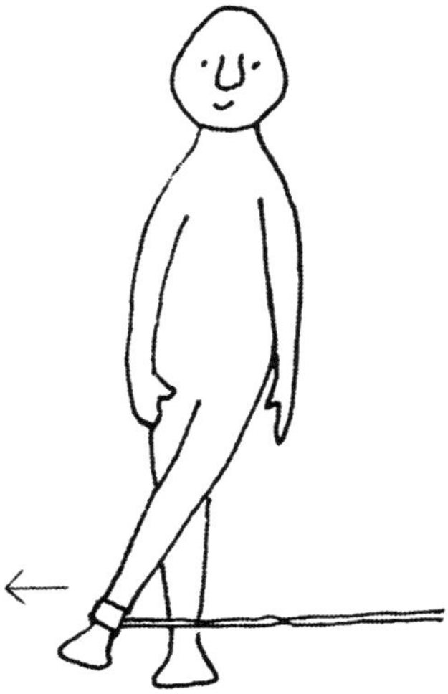

XI. Don't Be Pulling Strings

(hamstring stretch)

1. Lie on your back.
2. Lift one leg and hold the thigh just below the bend of the knee. Keep the other leg slightly bent.
3. Slowly straighten the raised leg until you feel a stretch in the back of your thigh.
4. Hold the position for thirty seconds.
5. Do the same procedure with the other leg.
6. Alternate legs, five times.

Do two times per day.

XII. Holding Up the Building

(wall slides)

1. Lean on a wall with your back.
2. Slowly lower your buttocks toward the floor until your thighs are horizontal.

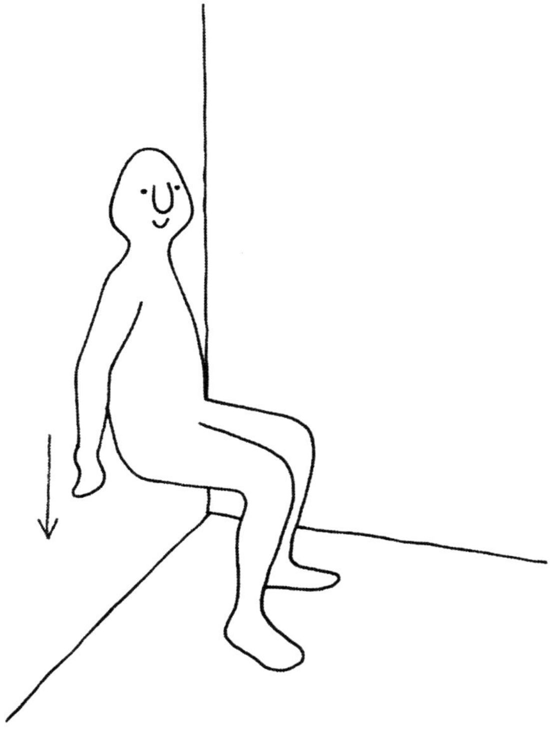

3. Hold for ten seconds.
4. Keep your thigh muscles tight as you slide back up to the starting position.

Do ten repetitions, two times per day.

XIII. Nodding Off

(neck stretch)

1. Gently bend your head forward, count to five, and then bring it back up.
2. Gently bend your head backward, count to five, and then bring it back up.
3. Gently bend your head to one side, count to five, and then bring it back up.
4. Gently bend your head to the other side, count to five, and then bring it back up.

Do the sequence ten times, two times per day.

XIV. Flex Your Wings

(elbow touches)

1. Sit down or stand up.
2. Touch your shoulders with your fingertips, the left hand on the left shoulder and the right hand on the right shoulder.

3. Lift your elbows to shoulder level.
4. Try to touch your elbows together in front of you or as close together as possible.

Do ten repetitions, two times per day.

XV. The World Is Tilted

(side leans)

1. Stand with your feet shoulder-width apart.
2. Make sure your knees are not locked.
3. Lean sideways as far as comfortable as your hand glides along your leg. Hold for five seconds.
4. Slowly return to your upright starting position.
5. Do the same on the opposite side.

Do ten repetitions, two times per day.

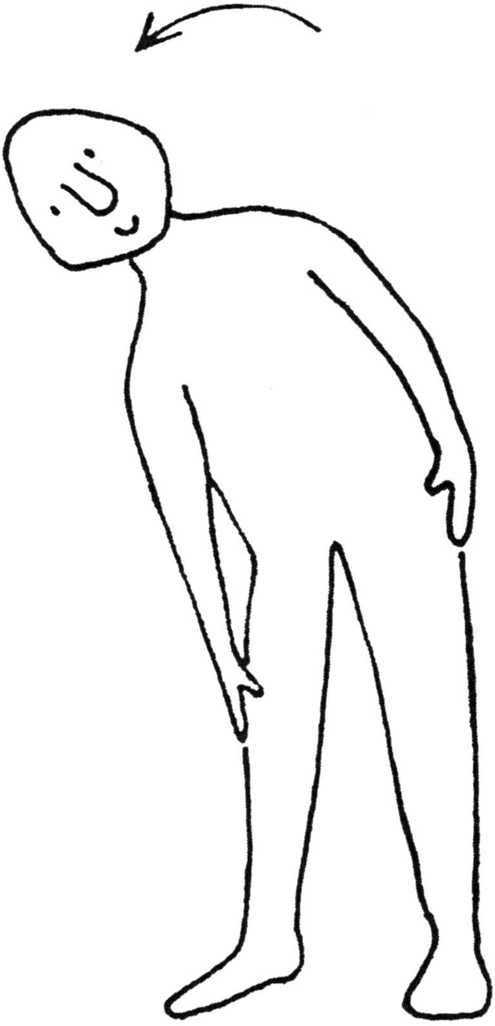

XVI. Squeeze Play

(back stretch)

1. Lie down and hold a pillow between your feet with one foot below the pillow and the other foot above the pillow. The pillow should rest on the top of the lower foot and under the bottom of the upper foot.
2. Squeeze the pillow between your feet as you slide the upper foot down and the lower foot up.
3. Hold for ten seconds.
4. Switch foot positions and repeat procedure.

Do ten repetitions, two times per day.

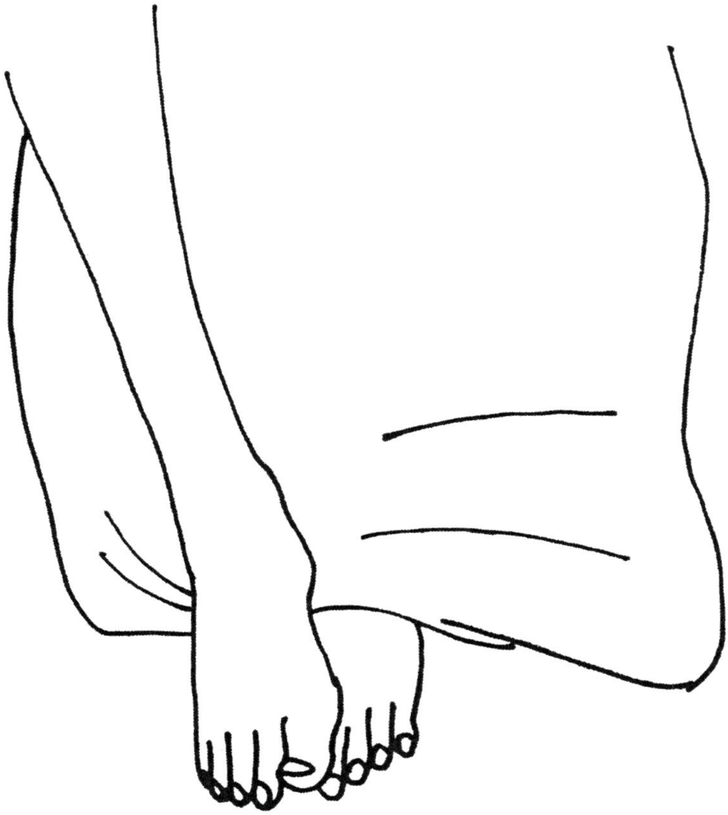

XVII. Rockin' Feet

(double toe raises)

1. Stand facing a table or other piece of sturdy furniture. Hold the table or furniture for support.
2. Push up onto your toes.
3. Hold for ten seconds.
4. Slowly bring your feet down and rock back onto your heels so that your toes are raised off the floor.
5. Hold for ten seconds.

Do ten repetitions, two times per day.

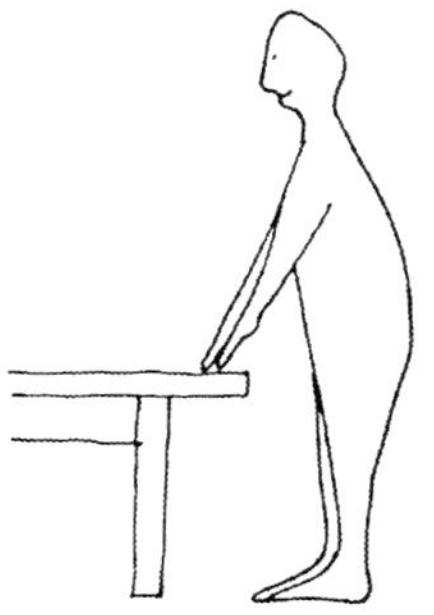

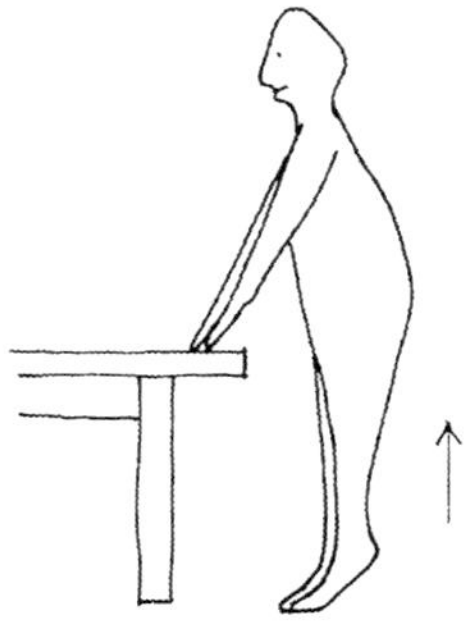

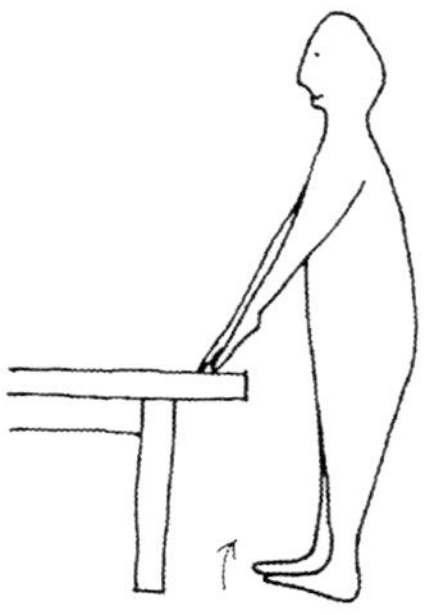

XVIII. Take Your Feet for a Spin

(ankle circles)

1. Rotate your ankle clockwise.
2. Rotate your ankle counterclockwise.
3. Flex your foot up and down three or more times.
4. Do same procedure with other foot.

Do ten sets, two times per day.

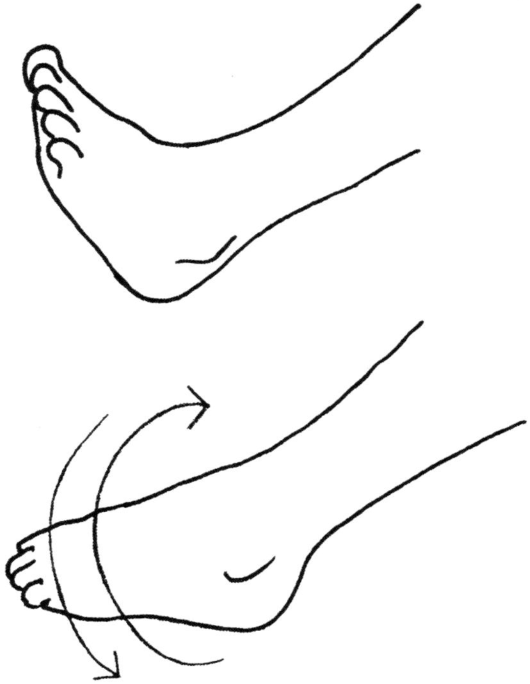

XIX. Restless Toes

(towel toe scrunch)

1. Sit down.
2. Place a towel under your foot.
3. Scrunch the towel up using the toes of one foot.
4. Spread the towel back out by relaxing your toes.
5. Now do the same with your other foot.

Do ten repetitions, two times per day.

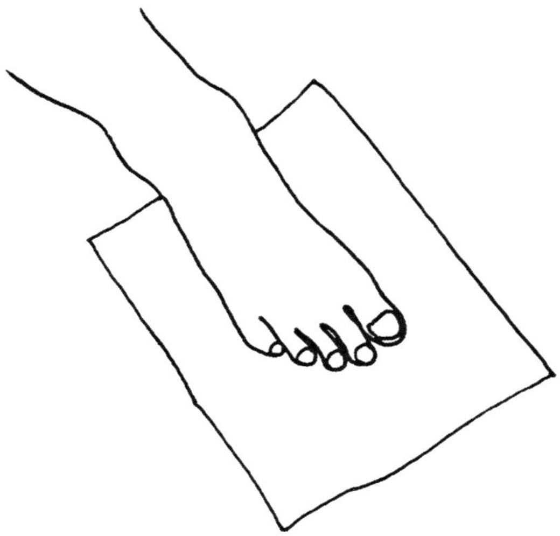

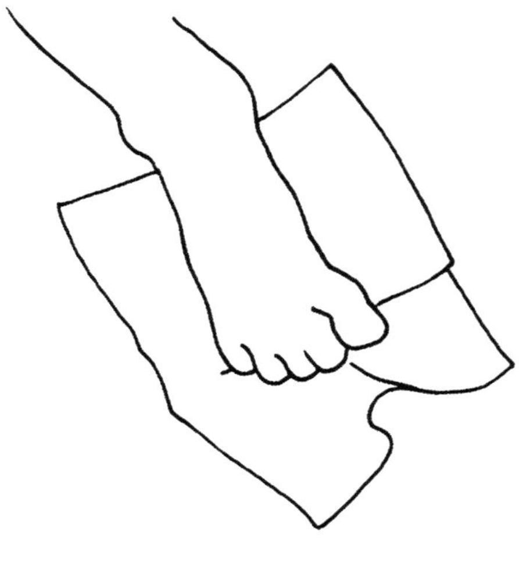

XX. Reach for the Stars

(body stretch)

1. Stand with your feet shoulder-width apart.
2. Put one hand on your hip.
3. Reach straight to the sky with the other arm. Hold for five seconds.
4. Now do the same with the other side of your body.

Do ten sets, two times per day.

SUMMARY: THE STORY OF MY LIFE WITH RHEUMATOID ARTHRITIS

My fifty-three volumes of diaries attest to the very active life I've led with rheumatoid arthritis.

There has not been a single boring or shut-in year. I was very much involved with my husband's office as well as my own businesses on the side. I was my husband's sole caregiver (except for some help in his last eight months) as he struggled with Alzheimer's disease. This care was physically demanding, and I often had very little sleep. During this time, however, I remained in good health and did not need to increase any medication for my RA, for which I must give credit to my diet and dietary supplements. (I am contemplating writing a book entirely devoted to my experiences as a caregiver to a victim of Alzheimer's disease.) I was also one of the most involved parents in my children's schools as they grew up. I've never given up sewing, piano playing, or helping those who come to me in need. All my life I've been an "arranger" of school drives, cruises, reunions, weddings, funerals, you name it. Many people have learned that they can rely on me. My relatives and friends have constantly kept me socially active. Work and love make my life rich and full.

Denial is not healthy. We rheumatoid arthritis victims must accept some limitations because of our condition. (For example, I would like to have enjoyed more sports activities.) Nevertheless, limitations never mean we should give up and take our sickness lying down. We should always be willing to help ourselves live an independent, happy life. My life has proven this possibility to be true. Believe me, if little Anita Chun can do it, so can anyone else.

It's been a very long and difficult journey for me to get where I am today. My exploration of conventional and unconventional treatments for this devastating disease has been tireless. I've had over a dozen surgeries—major and ambulatory—to correct or replace deformed joints. Now my rheumatoid arthritic condition is greatly improved and under control.

But I am not completely cured. I still need a minimum dose of RA medicine—but not enough to do me any harm. I adhere to the diet, supplements, and exercises I've found most effective over the years. The days I feel like shouting to the world how great I feel come more and more frequently now, and my gratitude to God keeps growing. I feel better now than I've felt since I was first attacked by RA over fifty years ago.

My main purpose in writing this book has been to share my experiences and triumphs with my fellow victims of rheumatoid arthritis. We don't have to be ashamed or embarrassed because we have rheumatoid arthritis. The disease is not a crime or sin. It does, however, sentence us to life imprisonment. But there are ways to parole ourselves from this prison. Together we can combat this terrible disease with phenomenal results. I am living proof. Am I so different? Don't we all have to learn patience, discipline, and tenacity in the end? My advice couldn't be simpler: "Think positive, think possibility, and *never* give up." My RA is about as severe as it gets, but even with all my pain in the early years, I've managed to live a happy, full life. I'd even say a normal life—but who's normal? No one! My hope is that my experience will give you shortcuts for finding your own kind of normal life.

It's taken me a long time—a lifetime—to find the best ways to deal with RA because I was trying every trial-and-error twist and turn, piling up research and analysis. I do not regret any of my efforts. Even the unconventional cures that didn't help taught me things about RA. Most important, they kept me away from the harmful drugs so often prescribed. In a way, the struggle to live healthy with RA can be boiled down to this simple goal: *Keep your dose of harmful drugs to a minimum.*

Surgery is always the last resort. Every surgery is a challenge. There are always risks involved (like infection), and the original joint will never be as good as new. But the increased mobility is wonderful. I've found surgery much more preferable to increasing the intake of strong drugs the rest of my life for joint pain relief. Too often with RA (and with other severe medical conditions), the disease doesn't kill the victim; the side effects of the drugs do.

Today, judging from my annual physical, I'm in top condition—despite RA and the hypothyroid condition I've had since junior high. My blood pressure is low, every organ healthy, and my blood tests excellent. I walk twelve or fifteen blocks a day when weather permits. Some days I walk twenty or thirty blocks. The weather no longer affects my joints, even in snow or high humidity. I do my own grocery shopping and cooking—which I enjoy a great deal. I have many friends and social activities. I still sew if needed. My son and daughter are as happily married to their spouses as Wei Foo and I were, and I have three lovely and bright grandchildren. My oldest granddaughter is a senior at

Princeton University and my second oldest granddaughter is a freshman at Kalamazoo College. My grandson is a sophomore in high school. My children are loving to me. Even though they live in the Midwest, we are in constant contact and get together for holidays.

I am my own day-to-day arthritis doctor. I have faith in God and myself. Faith leads to hope and strength. There is no room for self-pity. It is understandable to ask, "Why me?" when such a disease strikes. However, on analysis, we must realize that such a question can have selfish, even cruel implications: Do we want someone else to have it instead? The other side of this question is, "Why not me?"

It is sad that we have rheumatoid arthritis and that there's no cure yet. We all wish we were never stricken by it. But we are not in this alone. There are millions of rheumatoid arthritis sufferers in the world. There are over two million victims in the United States. It is a terrible disease, but not the worst. We still can do something about it to live a gratifying and productive life. The limitations are inconvenient at times—to say the least—but our creativity can always find a way. We can improvise with the best of them.

Before I conclude my story with RA, I must give credit to my late husband, Wei Foo, for his unwavering physical, mental, and emotional support during the darkest times. All those years I never heard him make a single complaint or ask for thanks. One day he even said to me, "The smartest thing I have ever done in my life is marrying you!"

The support from a spouse is the most valuable thing in the world to help the victim of rheumatoid arthritis. Such encouragement and devotion always lead to improvement. I am very lucky to have had such a blessing in my life as Wei.

I'm a fortunate, positive person, even with rheumatoid arthritis. I am sure that I am happier than many who are in perfect health. Over time, my resiliency has become a shield that keeps unpleasantness and sadness from hurting me. It is difficult to describe my inner peace and joy these days. Only people who have had such experiences can understand what I mean. It is my wish that every reader of this book and every rheumatoid arthritis victim will reach this plateau in the not-too-distant future.

I hope I am not being presumptuous by saying: Pain *was* my middle name, but now my middle name is *Triumph!*

ABOUT THE AUTHOR

Anita Li Chun was born in Shanghai, China, in 1924, the ninth child and the second daughter in a family of eleven children. She was a graduate of the renowned McTyeire High School for girls in 1943 and St. John's University in Shanghai with a BA in education in 1946. She came to New York City in 1947 for her graduate work at Teachers College, Columbia University, and received her MA in secondary school administration in 1948. She was stopped from completing her doctorate by rheumatoid arthritis at the age of twenty-five.

Over the years, she has pursued many conventional and unconventional treatments for this very crippling disease. Even though no cure has yet been found for RA, her never-say-die efforts in research and trial-and-error methods have led to a phenomenal improvement in her condition as well as her general health.

APPENDIX 1

REFERENCES

There are a number of good books and magazines about rheumatoid arthritis and general health and nutrition. The following are some of the core publications that the author reads.

BOOKS

Davis, A. *Let's Eat Right to Keep Fit.* New York: Signet, 1988.

Davis, A. *Let's Get Well.* New York: Signet, 1984.

Editors of Prevention Health Books, and A. Feinstein, eds. *Prevention's Healing with Vitamins: The Most Effective Vitamin and Mineral Treatments for Everyday Health Problems and Serious Disease.* New York: Rodale, 1998.

Gottlieb, B. *Alternative Cures: The Most Effective Natural Home Remedies for 160 Health Problems.* New York: Rodale, 2000.

Mindell, E., and H. Mundis. *Earl Mindell's New Vitamin Bible.* New York: Warner Books, 2004.

MAGAZINES

Arthritis Today.

Harvard Health Letter.

Johns Hopkins Medical Letter: Health After 50.

Mayo Clinic Health Letter.

Prevention.

Tufts University Health and Nutrition Letter.

APPENDIX 2

RETAIL SOURCES

The list below is provided solely for the convenience of the reader. The author has found the following products helpful for rheumatoid arthritis, and others have found them beneficial for other forms of arthritis. There is no financial association between the author and these retailers.

1. Aloe Vera capsules
Catherine's Choice
2421 Curry Ford Road
Orlando, FL 32806
1-800-330-2563 (24 hours a day)

2. Glucosamine Chondroitin, double strength (NOW)
Fruitful Yield Vitamins
P.O. Box 6247
Bloomingdale, IL 60108-6247
1-800-469-5552
www.FruitfulYield.com

3. Cordyceps capsules
R'Garden, Inc.
P.O. Box 417
Kettle Falls, WA 99141
1-800-800-1927 (Monday–Friday, 7:00 AM–5:00 PM Pacific Time)
www.rgarden.com

4. Sun Chlorella tablets
Sun Chlorella USA
3305 Kashiwa Street
Torrance, CA 90505
1-800-829-2828
www.sunchlorellausa.com

5. For some dietary supplements
Vitamin Shoppe
2101 91st Street
North Bergen, NJ 07047
1-800-223-1216 (24 hours a day)
www.VitaminShoppe.com
Vitamin Shoppe retail stores are located across the country.

6. For some dietary supplements
Puritan's Pride
1233 Montauk Highway
P.O. Box 9001
Oakdale, NY 11769
1-800-645-1030 (24 hours a day)
www.puritan.com

7. Walking shoes (*Free Time* style for women, *Time Out* style for men)
SAS Shoemakers
1717 SAS Drive
San Antonio, TX 78224
1-210-924-6561
Most shoe stores selling walking shoes carry the SAS brand.

978-0-595-34914-2
0-595-34914-5

CPSIA information can be obtained at www.ICGtesting.com
Printed in the USA
BVOW030121180412

287903BV00001B/42/A

9 780595 349142